WHAT I'VE LEARNED

Twenty-eight creatives share career-defining insights

FRAME

CONTENT

INTRODUCTION

'What I've Learned' is a successful section of *Frame* magazine that first appeared in May 2014. It's here that readers find the thoughts and opinions of designers and architects in articles that cover the experiences that have marked their careers. This eponymous book is a compilation of the 26 articles featured thus far in the pages of *Frame*.

Asking creatives to reminisce about their professional achievements is not so difficult in most cases, but having them recall their blunders is a different story altogether. Prior to the launch of 'What I've Learned', *Frame* experimented with two forerunners: 'Failures and Fortunes' and 'Éminence Grise'. These short-lived sections of the magazine appeared in four successive issues between September 2013 and March 2014. Practically speaking, 'Failures and Fortunes' focused far more on fortunes than on failures. After all, designers — like the rest of us — are not eager to point out their existential crises or their commercial flops. In 'Éminence Grise', the spotlight was on designers who greatly deserved the accolades bestowed upon them. Approaching the twilight of their careers, they turned out to be more open to self-examination and introspection than their younger colleagues, who had contributed to 'Failures and Fortunes'. Older designers tended to speak quite plainly about weathering the ups and downs of their profession and to be unafraid of criticizing clients, for example.

It wasn't long before the editors at *Frame* decided to merge the two sections of the magazine. The result is 'What I've Learned'. A stroke of genius, the section has become a go-to source of information and inspiration. Paging through the first few issues that included 'What I've Learned', you'll find that the editors did indeed choose older designers. Among the earlier interviewees was industrial designer Ingo Maurer (born in 1932), furniture designer Toshiyuki Kita (1942) and architect Tadao Ando (1941). As established role models, they empowered a younger generation of guests to express themselves more freely.

This compilation of in-depth articles provides a good impression of the challenges facing today's designers. The struggle between autonomy and commercial pressures, the sometimes problematic dealings with clients, the occasional feeling that the world is already overburdened with too much stuff: it's all part of the picture. But so is the high that comes with the discovery of something new, the freedom enjoyed by thriving independent entrepreneurs when selecting collaborators or partners, and the intense satisfaction of a well-designed product that's still popular years after it was introduced. Together, the various facets of a creative's activities make for informative reading of interest to every designer – and to everyone else. For one thing is clear: important life lessons have a universal value.

DAVID KEUNING

TADAO ANDO, who's well into his seventies, says he still aspires to create a 'masterpiece'

WORDS
Kanae Hasegawa

PORTRAITS
Madako Akiyama

TADAO ANDO

OPPOSITE PAGE **ATELIER IN OYODO II (ANDO'S OWN OFFICE), OSAKA, OSAKA, 1989-91.**

FOLLOWING SPREAD **MODERN ART MUSEUM, FORT WORTH, USA, 1997-2002.**

'I grew up in Osaka, in a district filled with family-run workshops and craftsmen. My after-school hours were spent with woodcarvers, glass-blowers and metalworkers, who took care of me and taught me their skills.'

'My grandmother raised me single-handedly. After my work had been featured in an architecture magazine, she passed away peacefully. She approached everything pragmatically. One of her theories was that it doesn't make sense to cart textbooks to and from school, so she ordered me to finish every assignment before leaving school each day, which meant I had no homework. People thought the idea was bizarre, but in the end I found it practical. She taught me that it's okay to be adamant about your beliefs as long as you find logic in them. This is something I've been exercising throughout my career.'

'At age 14, a seemingly small event made a decisive impact on my life. A second floor was being added to my house, and I saw a young carpenter working so incessantly that he even forgot to eat. I was struck by his attitude and commitment to the job; he ignited my interest in the world of architecture.'

'I wanted to study academically and train professionally, but I had to earn a living after school to support my grandmother. In addition, my school grades weren't quite high enough to study architecture at university. I begged my university-going friends for their architecture textbooks, which I read from cover to cover, cramming all the information students typically learn within four years into one. I also took a course in drawing via distance education.'

'Thanks to a couple of eccentric characters who showed an interest in someone with no academic training, I designed a club at the age of 18. Since then, my practice has evolved through trial and error.'

'I tell architecture students to travel while they're young — to experience historical architecture first hand. To me, the essence of architecture is the creation of a space in which people gather. I've felt it during my countless travels in Japan and overseas. It can be discovered in the

architecture of my famous predecessors, as well as in indigenous houses made by locals.'

'Early in my career, I realized that things hardly ever work out as intended. One of my first projects was a house for a couple with one child. As the house neared completion, the couple discovered they were expecting twins. My original plan was too small for a family of five. The couple joked that because I'm a twin [Ando has a twin brother], I brought them the same fate. In the end, I decided to keep the house as an office, and I still work there today.'

'Having experienced my own architecture as a user, I understand that architects are invariably responsible for what they create. As my studio took on more work, I had to make my office bigger; it's now five storeys high. I have no problem with the number of levels, but people arriving for meetings have to climb the stairs all the way to the fourth floor, as there's no lift. I've realized it's difficult to make architecture that serves everyone's needs.'

'Sometimes I underestimate how my buildings may be used in the future. My design of the Shiba Ryotaro Memorial Museum, which houses books by eminent Japanese author Ryotaro Shiba, incorporates an 11-m-high bookcase. Floor-to-ceiling shelves hold some 20,000 books that informed Shiba's writings. While the gesture is striking, the labour required to stack the shelves and clean the bookcase is something I should have considered earlier.'

'Regrettably, close consideration of the user is something I often neglect and only engage in after the fact. That's why I have all these models in my office. They're not of my projects; they're models of masterpieces designed by other architects, such as Louis Kahn, Norman Foster, Richard Meier and Arata Isozaki. I participate in many architecture competitions and often fail. But later I reflect on what was wrong with my plan, and why another architect's plan won. Being surrounded by models of famous buildings helps me to reflect. What keeps me going as an architect is the aspiration to make something close to — and perhaps that even transcends — these masterpieces.'

ABOVE **ANDO SURROUNDS HIMSELF WITH MODELS OF FAMOUS BUILDINGS AS A METHOD OF SELF-REFLECTION.**

OPPOSITE PAGE **ROKKO HOUSING, KOBE, HYOGO, 1978-83 (PHASE I), 85-93 (PHASE II), 92-99 (PHASE III).**

FOLLOWING SPREAD **SHIBA RYOTARO MEMORIAL MUSEUM, HIGASHIOSAKA, OSAKA, 1998-2001.**

'Having experienced my own architecture as a user, I understand that architects are invariably responsible for what they create'

Entrepreneur, humanist and sustainability advocate, **YVES BEHAR** believes that design is about questioning the status quo in order to move into the future

WORDS
Shonquis Moreno

PORTRAITS
Mark Mahaney

'I've always had a sense of the world, rather than a sense of nationality. When you're a designer you look at humans, and it's hard to be a designer if your view of the world is constrained by the idea of limits. Even as a kid, I never understood the notion of borders. In my work there's a lot of culture to be aware of − a lot of openness − and you have to be comfortable asking questions. Questions are the beginning of curiosity, and curiosity is the beginning of design.'

'Initially, I wanted to be a fiction writer. I went to a gymnasium where my imagination ran wild and I got into a world of storytelling. I wasn't very good at anything else at school, and writing was where I could excel − it gave me personal satisfaction. In my mid-teens, a teacher dissuaded me − he didn't think my fiction was good enough. I turned my attention to design, and it quickly became a way for me to tell stories. The idea that every object has a story to tell is something that I took to heart.'

'I wish that *talent* wasn't celebrated so much by design schools and that *work* was encouraged more. We tend to think of people having some sort of natural talent, as if it's God-given, but design is really about work *and* play.'

'Fuseproject has pioneered the notion of turning a client into a partner − we want to become totally integrated into our client's company. When that happens, our sense of responsibility, our thinking, our focus, our understanding of what's going to work and what's not − it's all sharpened to an incredible degree by the fact that what we're working on is not simply someone else's project. It's ours together − *ours* to make work, *our* success or *our* failure. What I look for in a partner is the belief that failure is not an option − the person has to be all in. A positive attitude convinces me that this is who I want to stand next to as we face the battles that are bound to come.'

'The real challenge for wearable technology is to make a product that's actually wearable. Since my partners at Jawbone and I created UP, the first wrist-worn activity and sleep tracker, many more players have entered

the field. A lot of them, however, try to include as much technology – and as many features – as possible, at the *expense* of wearability. People love personal data, insights and eureka moments that help them make lifestyle decisions. To get the most out of the data provided by such a device, it has to be worn 24/7. The success of our UP series lies in wristbands that are comfortable day and night, while *also* expressing a user's personal style.'

'One characteristic that helps me succeed is my tendency to fall in love with ideas – and to make others fall in love with ideas. When I get passionate about an idea and my client does too, we become partners in pursuit of a goal.'

ABOVE **PUBLIC OFFICE LANDSCAPE FOR HERMAN MILLER, 2013.**

OPPOSITE PAGE **SODASTREAM CARBONATION MACHINE, 2012.**

'The biggest myth is that sustainability looks a certain way, and another is that it doesn't require as much process, sophistication or capital investment. Thinking about a project with sustainability in mind depends on the market and the product. There's not just one criterion that makes a product sustainable.'

'Asking questions is one way to understand a problem, but it's also a way to let your mind wander through that problem. Every time I ask a question — and I'm always asking — it's an opportunity to bounce around an idea. It is the simplest way to learn and to get involved in a project at the same time.'

'Weaknesses and insecurities can be overcome. I used to be terrified to speak in public, but I worked hard to conquer that fear, and I got better at it. That's only one of many things that could be — should be — improved, but awareness of shortcomings shouldn't lead to self-hate. Being conscious of your problems makes solving them even more pleasurable.'

'When faced with a problem that still needs to be resolved, it's important for me to experience a feeling of being overwhelmed or confused. The problem has to sit in me, frustrate me, wake me up at night. Even though urgency and passion will be part of the resolution, I try to be patient. The balance lies in letting uncertainty and frustration be what they are, because such feelings motivate the brain to solve the problem.'

'I've never thought that great design can be done *only* when a great project lands in your lap. I took quite a few projects early in my career that some people would consider shitty. Most designers want to do a line of shoes, not the shoebox. But how long does that last? One season? Two? Whereas Puma ships 80 million shoes a year in the Clever Little Bags we designed for the brand, making that packaging system a long-term story. You don't need to design a car or a plane in order to make a difference.'

ABOVE **CLEVER LITTLE BAG SHOE BOX FOR PUMA, 2010.**

OPPOSITE PAGE **ELLIQ ACTIVE AGING COMPANION FOR INTUITION ROBOTICS, 2017.**

PREVIOUS SPREAD **YVES BÉHAR DESIGNED THE SAYL CHAIR FOR HERMAN MILLER, AN OFFICE CHAIR THAT INCORPORATES ENGINEERING PRINCIPLES USED IN CONSTRUCTING SAN FRANCISCO'S GOLDEN GATE BRIDGE.**

'I've never thought that great design can be done only when a great project lands in your lap'

ALEXANDRE DE BETAK rewrote the fashion-show playbook. Now he wants to apply his rebellious approach to more permanent fields

WORDS
Anna Sansom

PORTRAITS
Valentin Fougeray

ALEXANDRE DE BETAK

'I grew up in Paris in the 1970s and '80s and was influenced by the transition from *Dallas* and *Dynasty* to punk and the Clash in London, French New Wave and Japanese androgyny. I remember going through all those fashion phases and the momentum of *The Face* [magazine, 1980-2004]. At age 12, I had a darkroom in my brother's bedroom. At 15 I was taking pictures for Berlitz travel guides, and by 16 or 17 I was photographing Parisian nightlife for magazines. After high school, I enrolled at Sorbonne University and ran away a few hours later. I was impatient and wanted to jump into working. Later on I regretted not taking the time to learn such things as perspective drawing or software. But I don't regret the fact that I wasn't formatted to any set of rules that might have slowed me down. I've never learned any rules for what I do today.'

'I was 18 when I met Spanish fashion designer Sybilla and offered to help her. I did all her shows in Madrid, Milan, Tokyo and Kobe before she left the fashion world. After that I moved to New York, a city that was more multidisciplinary-minded than Paris. The mix of different things I was doing didn't have a name back then. I offered services around concept, creative direction and production, casting, and lighting. I came as a full package and did everything myself. I was 20. It worked. I was lucky.'

'There's a European snobbery towards Americans in terms of culture and creation. I thought the innovation in New York was great, but weirdly enough the results — especially in fashion — were not. But there's more freedom in America, which is linked to it being less ancestral, and that gave me the liberty to propose whatever I wanted. I had a deeply personal approach and a completely different vision.'

'I began doing extremely minimal, extremely architectural shows, which corresponded to what was happening worldwide, but mine were spectacular, narrative and performance-based. I did some of the early Prada shows and the launch of Miu Miu, which opened with Chloë Sevigny in New York in 1994. It was a stripped-back architectural set — white, with minimal music.'

Daniel Beres

'In the shows I did for John Bartlett, I played with homoeroticism and crazy casting with animals. It was the period of '90s grunge and Calvin Klein androgyny, and we cast butch guys with big moustaches, sitting on a boardwalk, as a counter-trend. I also started working with Michael Kors, transmitting his message about beautiful, sexy women.'

'I have no specific source of inspiration — unless you count everything. I've always travelled a lot and been curious. If I'm doing something performance-related, I don't look at other performances. Instead, I research artistic or architectural trends that interest me. If I embark on a new story with a designer or brand, I might think of doing something associated with kinetics and research that topic. Sometimes I start from nowhere, but I do know there's a mood I want to convey. There's no recipe for creative processes. I do most of my research on Google, although we have libraries in both Paris and New York. There's a great bookseller three doors down from me in Paris and a few other places nearby where I can research and relax.'

'Fashion is something I know a lot about. I've been working in the industry for 25 years, but it's never been the end in and of itself. My objective has been to create environments and experiences that leave long-lasting memories — it's about helping fashion brands and designers and making sure that fashion and luxury continue to be desirable. I've toyed with many subjects, learning specific technologies and studying historical periods and different cultures. I'm not interested in anything literal; I'm more about inventing and reinterpreting. Before I started working with John Galliano almost 20 years ago, he had a more literal, theatrical approach to communicating the inspirations behind his collections. I brought contrast to that. If a collection was based on a historical period, I tried to enhance it by proposing the exact opposite — as a way to create disruption.'

'Every creative relationship adds a layer to your life. Whether it's John Galliano, Viktor & Rolf, Hussein Chalayan, Raf Simons, Maria Grazia Chiuri [Dior], Anthony Vaccarello [Yves Saint Laurent] or Kate and Laura

ABOVE **ANTHONY VACCARELLO, AUTUMN/WINTER 2012, CITÉ DE LA MODE ET DU DESIGN, PARIS.**

FOLLOWING SPREAD **BERLUTI, AUTUMN/WINTER 2015, BY ALESSANDRO SARTORI, MUSÉE DES ARTS DÉCORATIFS, PARIS.**

Mulleavy [Rodarte], it's always a relationship of mutual exchange. They've shared their inspirations and great talent with me, and I've given them my interpretation in my proposals.'

'Of everyone I've collaborated with, Raf Simons is the most involved in his fashion shows. He understands all the stages that go into the final production. Like me, he has a completely free, open-minded approach. He can start out in one direction and shift 180° to another. Raf recently moved to New York. For his S/S 2018 menswear show, he wanted to re-create the energy that New York probably had before we were there. We felt this energy was best represented in the original *Blade Runner* film [1982], whose mix of futuristic yet raw aesthetics and extreme energy is a recurring inspiration for both of us, and for many people of our generation. The show was held late at night in an outdoor food market in China-town – no seats, only standing room. It was an incredibly short, messy setup. Minutes beforehand I was filling buckets with water and throwing it between people's feet to make sure the lights would reflect on the ground.'

'To make a show better, you need the ability to revisit whatever you had in mind – even during the event itself. No matter how great your idea is, it can always be improved if you allow yourself to modify it until the very end. Raf's show proved that you can generate amazing momentum without having everybody who's anybody there, since not all of the usual front-row audience went to Chinatown at 10 p.m. to stand in a wet food market. But they *did* see the experience through online images. That demonstrates how the typical parameters of fash-ion shows can be broken down. You can create an emo-tion for those who are there, which can be passed on to those who aren't.'

'Social media and Instagram have revolutionized how shows are done today. Before our time, photographers knelt at the edges of runways, shooting the girls from below. When I started, we moved the photographers to the front and changed the lighting to come from the front rather than the top. At the Armory in New York, a venue that's over 27 m high and nearly 55 m long, we

'YOU NEED THE ABILITY TO REVISIT WHATEVER YOU HAD IN MIND, EVEN DURING THE EVENT ITSELF'

OPPOSITE PAGE 'I'M NOT NOSTALGIC,'
SAYS ALEXANDRE DE BETAK. 'I'VE
ALWAYS BEEN INTERESTED IN THE
FUTURE AND IN TECHNOLOGICAL
ADVANCEMENTS.'

BELOW RODARTE, AUTUMN/
WINTER 2016, BY KATE AND LAURA
MULLEAVY, DIA ART FOUNDATION,
NEW YORK.

used lighting in a way that allowed photographers to shoot from far away. The internet, and everyone in the audience who has a screen in the palm of their hand, has forced a new viewpoint: absolutely everywhere. We've changed our approach to design and lighting so you can achieve what we call the "Instagram shot", and we make sure to provide designers and brands with the right conditions for that shot. We've adapted the timing and the choreography so that we can create emotion in live settings that might get relayed via hand-held devices with a few seconds of video.'

'At some point a mix of virtual and augmented reality will offer us 360° live views. We'll be able to choose what we look at. We've been trying out ideas using these technologies, which are costly and difficult at the beginning. In the future, you'll *feel* as if you're there, even if you're not. But I believe there will always be emotions that you

Alex Fradkin

can only feel in real life. The goal is to move people *at the show*, to affect all their senses and to create an emotion — the one aspect that is grander in a live setting. The new challenge lies in doing something that can only be felt live while also creating something that can touch one or two senses remotely. Shows will then have the freedom to change format, size, place and time. Maybe they won't have to be part of a traditional fashion-week schedule. You have to break the rules and change the tools.'

'What's interested me most about fashion is its need for nourishment from other creative media. More than simply being an adaptable guy — and without sounding pretentious — I like to think of myself as an intense participant in fashion shows and a person who's helping to create change.'

'I'm not nostalgic, and I've always been interested in the future and in technological advancements.'

'There's a lot more I'd like to do. We've just launched a collection of objects called Fashion Show Tools and Survival Gear [socks, headphones, baseball caps and the like], which is a mix of collaborations with brands. Recently I've designed a range of spaces for myself and others. Pluridisciplinarity is necessary today, and I can apply my personal creative approach to anything: the experience of a fashion show, the scenography of an exhibition, a piece of furniture, a light, an object — you name it.'

'I would love to continue to create, but to do so beyond the fashion world. The solutions that have worked for fashion and luxury should be looked at more by the worlds of technology, real-estate development and contemporary art. I'd like to do more permanent installations, too. Breaking boundaries between absolutely everything should allow everyone to do whatever they like — that's the world I'm lucky to be in.'

ABOVE **CHRISTIAN DIOR, READY TO WEAR, SPRING/SUMMER 2015, BY RAF SIMONS, LOUVRE, PARIS.**

OPPOSITE PAGE **SIMON PORTE JACQUEMUS, SPRING/SUMMER 2017, JARDIN DES TUILERIES, PARIS.**

From learning to sew to discovering American design: the **BOUROULLEC** brothers reflect on the encounters and influences that shaped their collaborative careers

WORDS
Melanie Mendelewitsch

PORTRAITS
Valentin Fougeray

RONAN AND ERWAN BOUROULLEC

1971
Ronan Bouroullec born in Quimper, Brittany, France

1976
Erwan Bouroullec born in Quimper, Brittany, France

1997
Spotted by Cappellini and commissioned for their first industrial-design projects

1999
Begin working together in Paris

2001
Hold first solo show at Galerie Kreo
Meet Rolf Felhbaum, president of Vitra, and work on new office system Joyn

2002
Stage the 'Ronan & Erwan Bouroullec' exhibition at London's Design Museum

2003
Publish their first monograph with Phaidon

2011
Mount the 'Bivouac' exhibition at Centre Pompidou Metz and Chicago's Museum of Contemporary Art

2013
Hold 'Momentané' exhibition at Musee des Arts Décoratifs in Paris
Unveil the Gabriel Chandelier, the first permanent contemporary piece installed in the Palace of Versailles

2015
Present '17 Screens' installation at Tel Aviv Museum of Art
Release Serif TV for Samsung

RONAN: 'Our grandparents were farmers from northern Finistère. DIY — home improvements and repairs — was part of their daily routine. Our parents weren't into manual labour, but they taught us a lot about things like making repairs and gardening. Ever since we were young, we've been tinkering away — it's something we taught ourselves to do.'

ERWAN: 'Ronan originally studied applied arts — first at Olivier de Serres [École Nationale Supérieure des Arts Appliqués et des Métiers d'Arts] and then at Ensad [École nationale supérieure des Arts Décoratifs]. Given our family background, it was easier to study design than to go to art school. It was a more recognized discipline, which had a clear purpose, while art was not as easy for some family members to understand. A few years later I went on to study fine arts at Cergy-Pontoise.'

'There are few women with whom we've developed products; engineers are most often men. When it comes to *textile*-related techniques, though, there are generally many female engineers, prototypers and so on. This echoes our family background: our father would look at a project from a structural perspective — he was doing heavy physical work with materials like wood and metal — whereas our mother taught us sewing and finer handicrafts. Women and men have a different approach to making, and I personally love the subtlety of the feminine way. It's linked with a better ability to concentrate.'

RONAN: 'Our four-handed approach began after we joined forces in 1999. Our relationship has evolved over the course of various projects. We've developed a greater maturity in our work. We've also managed to establish some sort of freedom. We used to confer and analyse our designs at every step of the way. Nowadays we work more independently, allowing things to grow before questioning ourselves.'

'We currently have a team of ten in our workshop. Erwan and I facilitate projects in much the same way as a conductor directs an orchestra. When one of us is hesitant about doing a project, that moment of doubt may lead to a more critical examination. Techniques and constraints are reassuring and form guidelines of sorts, but these are parameters that concern the maker rather than the user. Sometimes one of us is very much inside the project while the other maintains some distance, which allows him to see more clearly, because he doesn't get confused by the details.'

ERWAN: 'The real challenge of design is to learn how to distance oneself while maintaining control. The fact that we're a duo brings an almost schizophrenic dimension to our work.'

'We learned a lot from Giulio Cappellini. He's one of the first people who really listened to us and entrusted us with projects. I'm inspired by his intuition and by the way he's wrapped himself up in the Italian industry while maintaining a bold vision. He once told us that he never has bestsellers but *long*sellers. Many of his products weren't quick to sell but would find their "customer" later and establish themselves over a longer period. We've never forgotten this example.'

'Rolf Fehlbaum of Vitra also taught us a lot. In a way, you could compare him to a football coach; he helped us to improve and develop. When we started working together, he asked us to conceive office furniture, even though we'd never worked in a large office before. We were able to research an unfamiliar environment with an almost naive state of mind. As soon as we completed Joyn, our first product for Vitra, Rolf emphasized the need to maintain ingenuity. We continually try to follow his advice and keep a certain "unprofessionalism" and naivety in our practice. Everyone at our studio is young; it's often their first job.'

ALCOVE CABIN XTRA HIGH THREE-SEATER FOR VITRA, 2006-08.

'Prototypers, technicians and engineers have taught me a lot — but you have to collaborate with them in a subtle way. Some of them can be reluctant to oppose our vision or to tell us what they *really* think. They can be closed off and hard to move. I recently understood the need to envision a part of our work as a harvest of knowledge, techniques and flavours. If we can't hear or broaden a technician's opinions, the "harvest" idea is lost. There are many ways to do this, but simple handmade prototypes

and sketches often open up the discussion more than technical documents or 3D models can do.'

'It's impossible to work without an awareness of history. The older we get, the more we see design as a Darwinian phenomenon.'

'Because I studied fine arts, real design influences came to me later on. In a way, I have a polar view of design. I was impressed by the Americans, who had a joyful and positive way of addressing the largest audience through industrial production. Examples are Hans and Florence Knoll, George Nelson, Eero Saarinen and, of course, Charles and Ray Eames. Their work was typical of the American optimism of the '60s. Italian designers came later: Ettore Sottsass, Alessandro Mendini, Andrea Branzi and so on. Their punk approach was a real provocation against bourgeois common sense.'

RONAN: 'We're fascinated by the structure of vegetation. The organic — the logic and performance of the living — is so compelling. Plants often provide inspiration for structural research, although the results never try to mimic nature. But sometimes we seek some sort of opposition to constructed space — to the flat, orthogonal, monochromatic environment. We look for an almost animistic presence.'

ERWAN: 'The French culture was not quite ready for the emergence of design as a practice. It remains very marked by the *mobilier de style*, and for many design is just another contemporary "style". French manufacturers and craftsmen have begun to understand the purpose of designers and to see designers as people who conceive products with and for them. We're facing quite a terrifying no-man's-land here. In places like Italy and the Nordic countries, however, design is inherently part of the culture.'

'The fundamental role of design is to give shape to culture. When you visit a museum devoted to ancient civilization, design — more specifically: the shape of everyday tools, weapons, jewellery and the like — is often the only thing that remains. Being able to stand the test of time

ABOVE **CPH CHAIR FOR HAY, 2012.**

STEELWOOD CHAIR FOR MAGIS, 2007.

OPPOSITE PAGE **'MOMENTANÉ' AT THE MUSÉE DES ARTS DÉCORATIFS, PARIS, FRANCE, 2013.**

Paul Tahon

'THE OLDER WE GET, THE MORE WE SEE DESIGN AS A DARWINIAN STRUGGLE'

means that those tools are technically perfect and were useful, but on top of that you see the people *behind* them. You see their humanity and can determine, therefore, the shape of their culture.'

'The challenge is to re-establish a common understanding between manufacturers and users, as these two parties are becoming increasingly detached from each other.'

'Most of the companies we work with share a 1970s vision. It's home-oriented, based on sustainable domestic environments that barely change. When it comes to ecology, the idea of indestructible pieces of furniture that will last forever is essential. We don't want our objects to grow old or to be tied to a particular time period. The design of the '90s focused on screaming about deep change and a new aesthetic: a conception that gave birth to noisy objects that were too specific to age in harmony.'

'Alcove, a sofa for Vitra [2006-08], is one of our most successful projects, because it goes beyond the idea of a simple piece of furniture; it also organizes space. Alcove is the best summary of our Lit Clos [a sleeping cabin manufactured by Cappellini in 2000]; the concept is almost the same. But Lit Clos didn't sell at the time.'

'In our opinion, design can be shown in galleries, too. The gallery is an interesting place to remove oneself from the extremely rational framework of industrial production, to look for new paths or simply to express approaches that are too radical for large-scale production. Of course, since we're in a time of hyper velocity and the "starification" of designers, the legitimacy of the gallery can be questioned. In our case, though, we feel that the gallery is a necessary place to work — it goes hand in hand with the more traditional practice of product design.'

'For us, art feels like a surgical operation. Design, on the other hand, is akin to a form of homeopathy.'

OPPOSITE PAGE **NUAGE CANOPY AT PASEO PONTI, MIAMI, USA, 2017.**

Defying the commercial direction suggested during his formative years, DAVID CHIPPERFIELD says the most important aspect of his profession is a strong engagement with society

WORDS
Izabela Anna

PORTRAITS
Gene Glover

WHAT I'VE LEARNED

DAVID CHIPPERFIELD

1953
Born in London, United Kingdom

1976
Graduates from Kingston School of Art with a diploma in architecture

1980
Completes Part 2 of the architecture course at the Architectural Association, having finished Part 1 in 1975

1983
Designs a London shop for fashion designer Issey Miyake, which leads to opportunities in Japan

1985
After previously working at the practices of Douglas Stephen, Richard Rogers and Norman Foster, establishes David Chipperfield Architects, which now has studios in London, Berlin, Milan and Shanghai

1989-97
Designs and builds the River and Rowing Museum, Henley-on-Thames

2011
Receives the European Union Prize for Contemporary Architecture - Mies van der Rohe Award, and the RIBA Royal Gold Medal

2012
Directs the Venice Biennale under the theme 'Common Ground'

2013
Is awarded the Japan Art Association's Praemium Imperiale prize for architecture

2014
Completes Valentino flagship store in New York City

2014-16
Serves as artistic director of Italian furniture brand Driade

'When I started working independently as an architect in England in the 1980s, the conditions were difficult. There was a deep economic recession and, in comparison with the earlier post-war generation, not as many opportunities for young architects. Even to this day, architecture is more dependent on private commissions than on the public sector, and commercial clients are often distrustful of young architects. While in other European countries young architects were entering small competitions for schools and similar projects, in England at that time you had to make do with designing bathroom extensions for small houses. There was also a negative attitude towards modern architecture, led in some ways by Prince Charles.'

'The reason I eventually went to Japan to find better work was because my first real project in London was a shop for Japanese fashion designer Issey Miyake. Luckily, the financial boom in Japan coincided with the Japanese desire to bring designers and influences in from outside. The Issey Miyake shop in London gave me a chance to work for him in Japan, where for five years I participated in projects that weren't available to me in England.'

'There has always been phenomenal talent out there, but the problem with architecture education seems to be deciding which skills to encourage. Many architecture schools seem to focus on developing either conceptual skills or practical skills. Historically, you would say that German schools tended to emphasize the practical, and maybe not enough of the conceptual, whereas English schools were doing it the other way around. That might be a bit of a caricature, but it has some truth. ETH Zurich is often regarded as the best school of architecture, because it has always handled the balance between the conceptual and the practical very well. As far as an office is concerned, you need both qualities in your team. You want people who are good thinkers but whose thoughts can be channelled in practical ways.'

'I first studied at Kingston School of Art, which was more of a technical school, and I was encouraged to continue my studies somewhere more suited to my conceptual interests. A teacher at Kingston suggested that I might enjoy the Architectural Association [AA], where I actually became more practical. The people who taught me at Kingston *and* the AA were very encouraging and influential. I was hugely fortunate. I learned that teaching comes in many different forms, and the same goes for sources of inspiration.'

'At the AA, Su Rogers got us excited about modern architecture, about going to Paris, about seeing work by Le Corbusier and others who belonged to the early Modern Movement. She made me enthusiastic about architecture in a way that has lasted.'

'After completing my studies in the late '70s, I worked for Norman Foster and Richard Rogers just as their practices were becoming well established. It was a vibrant time, and those were exciting offices. Something I observed was the seriousness with which they approached their profession – and everything else, for that matter. In England, architecture had long been a rather amateur 'sport' for gentlemen; doctors, lawyers and architects all tended to come from the same kind of background. Foster and Rogers were part of the first generation to change the profession into something more dynamic, more outward-looking, more social – just think of the Pompidou Centre, a project that questioned what a social or cultural building could be. It was probably the last great utopian building. Looking back now, I realize more and more that persuading the authorities to approve a large-scale museum with such a radical appearance was an enormous achievement.'

CARMEN WÜRTH FORUM, BADEN-WÜRTTEMBERG, GERMANY, 2006-17.

'What I also learned during that time was that every detail of a building counts. They were obsessive about how a building fits together, how the services operate and how the structure works. Yet at the same time they were idealistic; they were children of '68. Details and idealism are the two main things I took from them – aspirations that continue to sustain me and my practice. How do you make architecture? How does architecture work at the most physical level? How does it engage users in the most social way? Making nice concrete buildings or designing nice window frames is not what architecture is about. It has to be engaged.'

Simon Menges

'It is a sad thing if architects can demonstrate engagement only through specifically cultural buildings. In England we've experienced a significant shift from the post-war situation, when architects worked on everyday schools and housing, not just museums. Their task was to build a new society. People of my generation have grown up in a more commercial environment, where clients often choose architects to help them make more money. We think we're contributing to a better world, but our commercial clients are pursuing a richer world. We would like to add quality; they want us to add monetary value.'

'We architects can no longer get up in the morning and say *let's build some social housing*, despite our deep commitment to society. We want to make a positive impact and to provide a service. Perhaps not the popular perception of architects, it's what drove me to direct the 2012 Venice Biennale under the theme "Common Ground". It was an attempt to show that architecture can have purpose only when it's an engaged, collaborative activity. The biennale marked a critical moment; unless we were to become more engaged with the social issues of our time, we would be nothing more than decorators. In many ways, that is what happened: "architecture" has been reduced to a special event or monument. People think of good architecture as a visual spectacle at the end of a pilgrimage. For me, good architecture should be the building on the other side of your street; it should be the school where you drop off your kids; it should be the norm. That is what we have tried to do with our office campus in Berlin. When designing the project, we seized the opportunity to take all the nonsense away — everything that might otherwise be found in a commercial office project — and to show that it doesn't have to be too expensive. Architecture can be simple and have value beyond the aesthetic.'

'Balancing the commercial viability of a practice and its intellectual ambitions is a struggle. As an office, we work on projects that may not have a strong commercial incentive but that are important to us, especially in terms of scale. Ideally, an office the size of ours would work only on large-scale projects, which are relatively easy to manage. If a project takes five years, you can guarantee

RIVER & ROWING MUSEUM, HENLEY ON THAMES, UK, 1989-97.

'People think of good architecture as a visual spectacle at the end of a pilgrimage'

Ute Zscharnt

a certain level of security and plan your time to good effect. You have breakfast, lunch and supper all lined up. Small-scale projects are more like snacks; you eat them without knowing when you'll be having your next meal. As a result, you tend to gravitate towards the long-term work, even though it slows the overall production of your office and means you won't get the quick feedback that comes with short-term jobs. Philosophically, we like the idea of building all kinds of typologies and taking advantage of a range of intellectual and creative opportunities. If an interesting client wants to build a very good department store, for example, why not accept the challenge? Whether we're engaged in a commercial, cultural or private project, we aim for an achievement of the highest quality.'

'Though I grew up in the countryside, I am still excited by urban life. Cities are an interesting phenomenon and one we have to address, but I believe we're currently in a state of crisis, especially in London. Problems affecting the built environment are more about planning than about architecture, but we need to play our part. I spend a lot of time in Galicia, and last year I began a study of the ecosystem there, including a qualitative assessment of the environment. I think the study I'm doing in Galicia is relevant to the way we look at cities. A great city depends on keeping the good things and changing or revitalizing the spaces in between. A city ought to be developed organically and intelligently. It's an issue we're addressing in Galicia, with an exercise that allows us to talk about quality of life and not just about architecture as an independent activity.'

'In Galicia, people appreciate the alignment of expectation and reward. Their sense of contentment seems to emerge from the region's beautiful scenery and their devotion to it. They may not be able to articulate what they feel, but love of place is in their blood. In the city, where buildings replace nature, architects have to design buildings that create a similar love of place — a meaningful relationship between inhabitants and their surroundings. You can't transfer the conditions found in Galicia to the streets of London, but you *can* hold on to the notion of quality of life and protect it.'

ABOVE **CAMPUS JOACHIMSTRASSE, BERLIN, GERMANY, 2007-13.**

OPPOSITE PAGE **VALENTINO NEW YORK FLAGSHIP STORE, NEW YORK, USA, 2013—14.**

The knowledge accrued by ILSE CRAWFORD during ten years in publishing set the foundation for her desire to create environments that mean something to their users

WORDS
Enya Moore

PORTRAITS
Winter Vandenbrink

ILSE CRAWFORD

1962
Born in London, United Kingdom

1989
Selected as launch editor for *Elle Decoration*

1998
Appointed vice president of Donna Karan Home, New York

2001
Establishes Studioilse in London
Founds Man and Well-Being Department at Design Academy Eindhoven

2015
Designs Sinnerlig collection for Ikea

'My interest in the way that space affects people started when I was very young and keenly aware of how we lived — a Scandinavian-inspired lifestyle, I guess you'd say. The big family and the "always space around the table" mentality were hugely attractive to people. The informality and warmth were like a magnet. Visiting other houses, which were more controlled, I was always aware that the temperature suddenly dropped by several degrees.'

'I had a left and a right brain growing up. My dad was an economist and my mother an artist. I learned very early on that they had two different languages and that getting things done meant talking to each other. That knowledge has been hugely useful, because one problem I often face is how to win the trust of my client. With interiors — jobs that can involve huge amounts of money and long timelines — gaining trust may require big leaps of faith. It is vital to work out how to win a client's trust and to communicate the intention.'

'My mum was quite ill for a long time, and I spent a lot of time in institutional environments. My eye became attuned to spaces that made people feel at ease with each other and to interiors that were positively detrimental. The difference wasn't necessarily about scale; some types of spaces are naturally more inhabitable then others.'

'My interest in interiors stemmed from the contrast of spaces that worked and ones that didn't, but also from magazines. Working for a magazine gave me a real on-the-ground education, an insight into what is actually successful. I saw so much *new* that I began to prioritize what would last and connect. I am still interested in the new, but I am also concerned about the relevant.'

'We can't keep talking about sustainability *and* constantly produce more stuff. It is human nature to try to renew ourselves completely, but I want the things that we do to add something useful to the list.'

'Starting *Elle Decoration* at 27 was terrifying. I was originally asked to do a supplement, which eventually turned into a bimonthly. There were four or five of us in the parcel room, all ex-art school, painting sets and packing

props. We felt strongly that there needed to be a magazine that felt alive and relevant to our generation, to the designers that we knew: the Toms, all those people who were children of a different generation. At the time, there was nothing that appealed to the young consumer. I did ten years in publishing before feeling that it was time to roll up my sleeves and leave the office. As an editor, I didn't get out that much – I wanted to move on to the physical stuff.'

'The publishing industry let me see and *feel* so much – very few designers have that opportunity. I learned the importance of communication, which should not be underestimated. It's about listening to your audience, understanding what their concerns are, and analysing what's going on out there before you do your thing. It is a discipline that comes from publishing. The world isn't waiting for you to deliver your idea.'

'In order to work with a client, designers need to really understand how a space is going to operate and evolve. There are moments when a client changes their mind in the middle of the project, and that's tricky. It's like being asked to make a church Catholic, only to be told to make it Protestant halfway through. The final result ends up being inarticulate.'

'Our best spaces have been realized when we've had the opportunity to understand the use. What concerns us most is the aspect of wellbeing. When we were asked to design the Cathay Pacific lounges, we sat and watched people's behaviour. Passengers have to perform the second they are off the plane, when most of them are just dog-tired. They want to shower, sit, eat, do their digital bit, and exhale. It's all well and good inserting great furniture, but what people need most is privacy. Many travellers make a ring of airport carts around their chairs to create a bubble for themselves – a physical bubble that reflects the digital bubble. So we gave them artificial bubbles. The important thing is understanding users' needs and designing spaces that respond to those needs.'

'Wellbeing represented a gap in the industry when Design Academy Eindhoven asked me to start the Man and Well-Being department. I was chosen for my interest in the combination of wellbeing and design, which wasn't shared by many others at the time. It's a much hotter topic now. How do you put warm values into a cold system? If you want to move a company forward, wellbeing has to be evidence-based. Ideas need to be quantitative and written in an Excel sheet, but how do you get unmeasurable things into society?'

'IT IS VITAL TO WORK OUT HOW TO WIN A CLIENT'S TRUST AND TO COMMUNICATE THE INTENTION'

'As a teacher or coach, you tend to offer certain pieces of advice, one of which is to follow the process, step by step. Don't try to get to the end *before* completing the stages in between; you'll limit yourself and likely miss huge opportunities. Just following the correct steps can take ideas to amazing destinations. What ends up as a real breakthrough is certainly the result of process, work and reflection. What I'm offering is a tool to get you to the end. My other piece of advice is: you just have to work.'

OPPOSITE PAGE **ILSE CRAWFORD:
'WE CAN'T KEEP TALKING ABOUT
SUSTAINABILITY AND CONSTANTLY
PRODUCE MORE STUFF.'**

BELOW **BEING HUMAN CABINET FOR
ZANAT, 2017.**

Martyn Thompson

'There is no such thing as design any more. There are so many channels to pursue. To achieve something really interesting, you've got to be able to work with people from other disciplines. That's when the real breakthroughs occur. Other fields are where design has a purpose. It needs to be engaged with something beyond itself.'

'Every project presents a steep learning curve. The best results come from working with people in a certain genre. That is the exciting bit about what we do — learning about something that you would never have imagined.'

'Tight restrictions test designers, but that makes it interesting. For our collection with Ikea we worked very closely with different suppliers to understand how we could use materials to their best advantage. For the cork pieces we worked with a historic Portuguese cork supplier that have transformed their production following the decline of wine bottle corks. They invested heavily in research and technology to understand cork's potential and develop an impressively sustainable, closed circle production system to ensure almost nothing gets wasted. Any leftovers are ground down into an ever-finer powder that can have another use elsewhere. Their survival is based on research and development and there are thousands of jobs at stake.'

'The Ikea project challenged our basic principles in a way. The company came to us because the collaboration was so unlikely — or maybe likely? Apparently, Ikea really likes designers who work with natural materials. The possibility of taking tactility and human feeling to a bigger audience at reasonable prices was hugely interesting. It meant a big learning curve for us, working within such a demanding and smart system. There was a university of knowledge there.'

'Every assignment is interesting in its own right. The projects I have particular affection for are the ones whose clients really look after them. Returning to a project where the clients really use and *love* what we've created gives me a great feeling. It's the most rewarding thing in the world to see something that didn't exist before now busy and alive with people. That is my litmus test for projects.'

Treading the boards as a bassist in an '80s funk band, **TOM DIXON** developed an attitude that he has applied to design and business ever since

WORDS
Enya Moore

PORTRAITS
Andrew Meredith

WHAT I'VE LEARNED

TOM DIXON

'I went to Holland Park Comprehensive — a somewhat rough school in central London. It was miserable in terms of formal education, but we had quite a good art department. The pottery course I took was probably quite instrumental for me. I learned that I could turn a piece of mud into an object of desire.'

'I discovered guitars when I was 14 or 15, and I was in a band after I left school. I tried a few jobs. I was a printer. I coloured in cartoons — when they were still coloured in by hand. Then the band took off, and I worked as a musician for a couple of years. Design, as a profession, wasn't something that even crossed my horizon. It wasn't a career that I was even remotely interested in.'

'The music business has a completely different set of rules. My experience was definitely coloured by the fact that I started to realize you didn't really *need* a certificate in music to be a musician. It's that sort of the attitude that I've taken into everything since.'

'Speed of delivery taught me how to be a designer. I was really crap when I started, but things gradually became more polished — and the welding got better.'

'The S-Chair came through a series of experiments. It started with the sketch of a chicken, but the end result was nothing like a chicken. Cappellini transformed the S-Chair from a rough, rubber-tyre tube chair into the much slicker model that exists now. That's when I started learning about design proper.'

'The S-Chair ended up in MoMA — a place that designers are obviously desperate to get into — but I didn't realize it was that important. I quite liked being in the V&A, though, because it was somewhere I visited a lot as a kid.'

'The Italians were amazing. It was never an issue that I was not a trained designer. They spotted what they wanted and formed relationships with people who loved design. In England, nobody *loved* design. Nobody cared.'

'In Italy, they wanted to make your design better. It was a revelation. I never felt even remotely out of my depth.

I felt supported for the first time. I discovered this rich and wonderful world where decisions were not based on purely commercial considerations. They were made over a delicious lunch in the factory with the family — and the grandmother popping in to give her opinion. It was really warm, and the complete opposite of London.'

'I have taught in art schools and noted that students often hear things like *no, you can't do this, it's not correct, try another one*. It wasn't like that for me. I would make something and if I didn't like it, I'd cut it up, sell it and make another one. I got better by practising.'

'A lot of designers misunderstand the role of manufacturers. They view production as advertising and communication. They think they're going to make innovative design objects and earn lots of money, but in reality the more extraordinary the object, the less likely it is to sell.'

'The Jack Lamp was my first plastic product. I founded Eurolounge to produce it, and it was then that I became conscious of trying to do things differently instead of just being swept along in a tide of events that were out of my control. The company represented my move out of metalwork to manufacture a product that could be made and distributed industrially.'

'Anything that pushes me in a different direction is significant. I hated scented candles when I was at Habitat — I always thought they were beneath me. But my involvement in perfume and fragrance has opened a whole other world with a different type of expertise. It's made me realize how important that intangible stuff is.'

'I think the most important skills are the peripheral ones. For me, the interesting people are the ones who are good at mathematics or project management — or who've simply had a proper job, like a nurse. If you can do something like that, you can do anything.'

'I'm not particularly interested in the design component of my work. I spend a lot of time trying to get people to *un*design. I don't want jazzy shapes that can turn into glass at the touch of a button.'

ABOVE **S-CHAIR FOR CAPPELLINI,** 1991.

JACK LAMP FOR EUROLOUNGE, 1994.

FOLLOWING SPREAD **OFFICE LOBBY AT SEA CONTAINERS HOUSE, LONDON, UK, 2014.**

Peer Lindgreen

'I like the whole chain of events, from raw material to design to a product that people are prepared to shell out cash for. I think all designers want to make money, but they may not want it as much as other people do — or they may not stop to consider what people are willing to pay for.'

'Be yourself. The most important thing in the modern world is to have a unique attitude. People aren't interested in me-tooers or versions of something else. They're attracted by the personality of an object and by something that's different from what's already out there.'

'There is a benefit to the open source model, but it's difficult for designers to mature enough within an aesthetic before having their ideas dumped and being forced to move on to the next thing — as a result of having revealed all their cards. It is increasingly tough to find that moment when you are *not* known. I quite like privacy. I had the advantage of being anonymous for a while.'

'I never look at my work and think: *oh, that's perfect.* I always think: *oh, fuck it. If only I had just…* And then it's too late. I see faults in every single object.'

'Young designers should seize the moment. Don't ask for too much advice. Try not to care too much about what other people think, because it's not useful. In the modern world, you can get destroyed very easily on Twitter. The thing is to just get on with it.'

'I don't have any intrinsic skills; I just practised. I think the virtual world provides an amazing opportunity, but it's dangerous to churn out ideas and never make them.'

ABOVE AND OPPOSITE PAGE
MONDRIAN HOTEL AT SEA CONTAINERS HOUSE, LONDON, UK, 2014.

FOLLOWING SPREAD **MCCANN ERICKSON ADVERTISING AGENCY OFFICES, NEW YORK, USA, 2014.**

Only while working in the United States did NAOTO FUKASAWA become aware of his Japanese roots

WORDS
Kanae Hasegawa

PORTRAITS
Tada (Yukai)

NAOTO FUKASAWA

1956
Born in Yamanashi
Prefecture, Japan

1979
Graduates from Tama
Art University and starts
working for watch
manufacturer Seiko

1989
Starts working for ID TWO
(now IDEO) in the United
States

1998
Establishes IDEO Japan

2003
Founds Naoto Fukasawa
Design

2007
Receives the title of Royal
Designer for Industry from
the British Royal Society
of Arts

OPPOSITE PAGE **ISSEY MIYAKE STORE GINZA, TOKYO, JAPAN, 2017.**

BELOW **HARBOR ARMCHAIR FOR B&B ITALIA, 2017.**

'In 1989 I left Japan for the United States, after working as an in-house designer for Seiko Epson. I was attracted by the working environment of ID TWO (now IDEO), a design company in San Francisco that I first read about in a magazine. The firm was very progressive. In the 1980s, it was already involved in interaction design and had engineers and designers working hand in hand. Their office was really impressive. I'm convinced that good working environments play a significant role in producing beautiful items. Nowadays, many companies embrace this approach and make sure their offices are attractive, but in the '80s that was rare.'

'Back then, it was a revelation to discover that the project comes first and that a staff of designers would be appointed only after a goal is established. Companies like Apple were formed on this basis, and they proved how a project-centred organization can bring about significant design. This was very different from how most Japanese manufacturers worked at the time. In Japan, the organization came first. Working in a fixed configuration, the staff was expected to initiate new projects. I suppose a project-centred approach is similar to making films, where talents are gathered from different fields each time a new film is made.'

'Only when I was in the States did I realize that Japanese aesthetics and mentality are different from those in the West. Working among designers from diverse cultural backgrounds, I felt the need to know more about who I am myself and about what Japanese designers can contribute to the world. I spent many hours learning about Zen, the tea culture and the aesthetic concept of *iki*. I also studied the work of Japanese designers like Isamu Noguchi, Issey Miyake and Shiro Kuramata.'

'After working in the States for more than seven years, I felt it was time to return to Japan. Having gained a certain recognition in the States, I started to feel conscious of becoming famous in Japan. I was rumoured to be this "Japanese designer working overseas". This type of acknowledgement wasn't necessarily rewarding. I wanted to be recognized simply as a designer, not as a Japanese designer who is successful in the States.'

'I TRY TO GIVE OBJECTS A SHAPE THAT MANY PEOPLE CAN FEEL EMPATHY TOWARDS'

'Being in the States allowed me to appreciate Europe's design culture as well. I admire the European way of cultivating strong and lasting relationships between designer and manufacturer. It takes a long time to establish such a relationship. However, once a designer becomes part of a company's family, the relationship will generally last.'

'Being in Silicon Valley in the 1990s was crucial for my career. Technology changed the way home appliances look. Until then, computers and other appliances had to be rather voluminous, in order to accommodate all necessary mechanisms. Technological advancement in the '90s allowed appliances to become smaller. Apple led the way. In the future, objects will almost disappear.'

'Physical objects will become less prominent as they become more compact. What matters is an object's

BELOW **SAIBA MULTITASK CHAIR FOR GEIGER, 2015.**

PLUS MINUS ZERO HUMIDIFIER FOR PLUS MINUS ZERO, 2003.

SIWA BRIEFCASE FOR ONAO, 2009.

OPPOSITE PAGE **NAOTO FUKASAWA'S PORTFOLIO INCLUDES WORK FOR CLIENTS SUCH AS ARTEMIDE, B&B ITALIA, LAMY, MAGIS AND THONET. HE IS A MEMBER OF THE MUJI ADVISORY BOARD, AND CHAIRMAN OF THE JAPAN FOLK CRAFTS MUSEUM.**

FOLLOWING SPREAD **HOMME PLISSÉ STORE BY ISSEY MIYAKE, TOKYO, JAPAN, 2016.**

Hidetoyo Sasaki

relation to its surroundings. Users look for atmospheric pleasure; an object's user experience can win consumers' hearts. That's why my focus nowadays is more about rendering a certain atmosphere.'

'I try to give objects a shape that many people can feel empathy towards. When I started as a designer, I was always trying to find a way to legitimize my work. I was obsessed with *my* design, but I now realize that people aren't interested in *my* work. I am not an artist. As a designer, I need to look around and observe how and in what settings people use items like teakettles and chairs. Observing the many ways that people use objects helps me to figure out the common aspects of human behaviour.'

'Fifteen years ago I founded my own company, Naoto Fukasawa Design. Currently, I have a staff that varies in size from eight to 11 designers. I encourage my staff to become independent and to start their own offices at some point. I like to follow the way that film-makers approach their work. I ask my designers to help me out on projects I'm responsible for, aside from the projects they're doing on their own.'

'When commissioned to make a design, I used to propose several ideas to my client, even if I preferred one idea above the others. Once a client chose the idea that I felt least confident about. Obviously, the project didn't go smoothly. What I learned from the experience is that, generally speaking, only one idea truly matches a client's brief. From then on, I presented the idea I felt was best. If the client isn't convinced, however, it doesn't necessarily mean the end of the project. I try to find common ground between the client's objectives and my understanding of the project.'

'With objects becoming increasingly smaller and occupying less space, my role as a designer is to think about design in relation to its surroundings. The relation ship between the object and its surroundings — the ambient — is just as important as its shape.'

His Latin designs in Germanic Switzerland made Buenos Aires-born ALFREDO HÄBERLI an outsider – and brought him great success

WORDS
Lilia Glanzmann

PORTRAITS
Mirjam Kluka

'One of my cherished childhood memories involves playing with Matchbox cars and then counting them before carefully putting them away in a little pouch. That was my world — the world I liked best. Even today, I don't know why I liked my turquoise car most of all: the attraction was tremendous, and still is. When I moved to Switzerland from Argentina as a teenager, the sole thing I packed was my little bag of cars, even though I'd stopped playing with them by then. The turquoise car was an Iso Grifo Rivolta, whose shape — purely coincidentally — was drafted by my idol, Giorgio Giugiaro, at Bertone Studios. Later, the Iso Grifo grille inspired the backrest of my Segesta chairs for Alias.'

'Even though I had to learn German to attend the Zurich School of Design, I did manage to acquire my diploma as a product designer. Someone else might have stopped going to school or just given up entirely. The challenge triggered the opposite in me. I thought: *I'll show you*.'

'Born in Buenos Aires, I didn't know anything about Swiss design. Maybe that explains why I became such a fan of its history.'

'I'm a big admirer of anonymous objects — objects created simply to fulfil a function or a specific need, or to express joy or passion. The drawers, pinboard and shelves of my studio are full of such objects: the wooden seat of a rowing boat, a rubber glove for gardening, a Japanese toothbrush. Together with art and fashion images, they create and stimulate my world of colour and form. I have a book of collages — colours, compositions, abstract imagery — that I've collected without rhyme or reason. When I'm developing a range of colours for a fabric collection or an interior, I use these collages to achieve harmony or contrast. It's all about a feeling, a mood.'

'During my first visit to the Milan Furniture Fair in 1985, I experienced the craziness that is the design industry. There was no internet; there were no smartphones. Design guides were rare. I got information by talking to people, even without knowing their names or the names of the exhibiting companies. I just walked around

'I LEARNED A LOT FROM THE ITALIANS'

looking, constantly wondering where I should go and what I should see. I had a fantastic three days. You could ride in the dark-blue limousines, even as a student. From then on, I went every year.'

'When I got back from Milan, I wrote down the names of the companies I liked. It was my dream to work for them one day. When I talked about it at school, my teachers made remarks like: "Hang on, those are *trendy* things — consumer goods." Such designer objects weren't well-known in Switzerland. They were clearly postmodern — quite a contrast with what we were learning at the Zurich School of Design. I didn't understand the work I'd seen in Milan, but that's why it was appealing. I wanted to make sense of it. Today I'm working for almost all the companies whose names I noted in the 1980s.'

'I loved the library of the Museum für Gestaltung. I spent every spare minute there. I knew — and still know — every book on the shelves. I've read every issue of *Domus*, from the beginning.'

'I learned a lot from the Italians. Achille Castiglioni is definitely one of my idols, as are Bruno Munari and Enzo Mari.'

'My parents were working for Swissair, and we children could fly for free. I remember my parents saying, "Alfredo, books are important, but you'll learn from experience." So I travelled a lot as a student — one week in Barcelona, the next in London — forging contacts in the international design world.'

'Since becoming a father myself, I've learned to trust my instincts even more — as children do.'

'I set up my studio one week after graduation. My first assignments came five years later, from Alias, Driade and Zanotta. My Swiss colleagues and the local industry didn't approve of working for foreign companies at that time. It was taboo — they were convinced that "the Italians don't pay you". Hannes Wettstein and I were pioneers in that respect.'

OPPOSITE PAGE **HÄBERLI'S ZURICH STUDIO IS FILLED WITH 'ANONYMOUS OBJECTS', WHICH HE SAYS 'CREATE AND STIMULATE MY WORLD OF COLOUR AND FORM'.**

FOLLOWING SPREAD **HAUSSICHT PREFAB MODEL HOME FOR BAUFRITZ, ERKHEIM, GERMANY, 2016.**

'Designing is yet another way of finding out about ourselves'

'I CAN ONLY WORK WITH PEOPLE I LIKE'

'Certain ideas can be pursued only if manufacturers let themselves be persuaded by the impossible. And such manufacturers can still be found in Italy.'

'Because I can only work with people I like, I've learned to be brave enough to say no — something I never thought would be so difficult.'

'I stopped explaining products, which is what we did at design school. What was your thought process? What was the intention? Nowadays, I say the product has to speak for itself. It's something I learned from the Italians. They look at it and either they like it or they don't. They don't ask about the *idea* the way that Germanic people do. *Che bello* is enough.'

'I've learned to tell the truth about a project — even if it's very hard to do sometimes and even if it hurts.'

'Maybe my naive approach has led me to success.'

'When I met Jasper Morrison and Konstantin Grcic, I related to them on a personal level — it was an experience that came quite naturally.'

'When I have a design block, I often flip through cartoon books. They reactivate ideas, relax my mind and bring a smile to my face. There are commonalities between cartoons and my work: leaving things out, achieving maximum communication with minimum strokes — and, when it makes sense, even without words. Just like design, cartoons are about lines, optimization and economy of media. My thoughts find a place in small sketchbooks or on notepaper. Perhaps I'll compile them in a small book one day.'

'I spend one to three days a week travelling, mostly just day trips, but occasionally I stay overnight. You arrive somewhere, hop in a taxi, head straight to your meeting, and then it's off to your hotel — or maybe to dinner somewhere in town. The next day, it's the same thing all over again.'

'Travelling is one reason why I never taught students in the past — it takes time. The other reason is that I'm hard on my colleagues who teach. I think it's a disaster if they teach just because they didn't make it as designers themselves. You need practice and experience in the industry to teach students; otherwise, it's always some kind of sheltered workshop. Now that I finally have time, I've decided to share my knowledge with the younger generation and will be teaching a masterclass in Basel.'

'In my role as a teacher, I want to ask questions that will provoke and motivate my students to enter uncharted territory. I'm excited about hearing their answers. I hope to see ideas with a strong character and a potential for becoming unique and distinctive products.'

'Being able to work and make a living as a designer is wonderful. I hope that as many young people as possible will have the opportunity to share that dream.'

'It's important to have the courage to *move* towards your good fortune. In my case, it meant taking the train to Milan. Keep dreaming. And afterwards: keep working.'

'Money never comes first.'

'People imagine that my images emerge from some deep-seated source of inspiration – that everything falls into my lap. But that's just how it looks. It seems easy to outsiders because I love what I do from the bottom of my heart. But in the meantime, I'm working as hard as hell.'

'What interests me is the variety, brilliance, innovation and surprising nature of contemporary products. As for my work, I try to observe and, in the process, to learn – from everyday life and from the people around me. As a designer, I look at the application of a particular technology or material in terms of its potential as a new typology. Is it original? Does it relate to traditional handicraft? And, also important, has it been done in a caring way?'

'Ultimately, I believe that designing is yet another way of finding out about ourselves, of carrying out in-depth examination and, not least, of discovering new things – as I did as a little boy with my Matchbox cars.'

STAMMPLATZ CHAIR FOR QUODES, 2017.

SPIN CHAIR FOR DURLET, 2006.

JAIME HAYON talks about happiness, mistakes and open dialogue — and about how his designs are a product of all three

WORDS
Matthew Hurst

PORTRAITS
KlunderBie

JAIME HAYON

1974
Born in Madrid, Spain

1997
Graduates in industrial design at the Instituto Europeo di Diseño in Madrid
Joins the Benetton-funded design and communication academy Fabrica in Italy

2000
Sets up own studio practice

2003
Quits Fabrica and dedicates himself fully to his personal projects
Exhibits for the first time, at 'Mediterranean Digital Baroque' in London's David Gill Gallery

2006
Elle Deco International Award

2008
Guest of honour at Belgium's Interieur Biennial

2009
AD Russia Designer of the Year

2010
Maison Object Designer of the Year

2012
Second Elle Deco International Award

2013
Designs his first wristwatch collection for a new Swiss watch brand Orolog

OPPOSITE PAGE **HOPEBIRD LIMITED EDITION FOR BOSA, 2012.**

FOLLOWING SPREAD **HAYON AT HOME IN VALENCIA, WHERE HE RUNS HIS STUDIO WITH A TEAM OF SIX. 'I HAVE FALLEN IN LOVE WITH VALENCIA. THE CHAOS INCREASES MY CREATIVITY.' A SECOND TEAM OF SIX IN TREVISO GIVES HIM THE 'CORE' HE NEEDS TO TACKLE ALL SORTS OF PROJECTS.**

'I grew up in Madrid, studied in Paris, worked for years in Italy with Fabrica before spending three years in Barcelona and five years in London. Now I live in Valencia. I have fallen in love with it. It's peaceful yet wild, a bit like Napoli. The chaos increases my creativity. I've evolved a lot in recent years.'

'My studio — with a staff of six — is at the centre of the city. I also run an office in Treviso, with another six people. With this core, I expand as needed to deliver each project. I could take on more people if I wanted to. The potential to grow is there. But for what purpose? I'm not a corporate guy. I take on the jobs that I want. That's richness to me.'

'As part of the international design scene, I get a lot of offers. But I'm constantly "curating" those offers. It's not about money, because these days there's enough work *and* enough money. I take projects for the challenge. There's nothing better than something you haven't done before.'

'I have a clear philosophy. I work with people I like. Whether it's a client or an artisan, I want to work with people I can commit to, and who can commit to me. I don't just respond to a brief. That's boring. That's the old way of design. Today it's about a dialogue. It's *me and you*. It's your day, it's my day, it's our wine, it's this moment. Good design comes out of doing things in a pleasurable way — with an open dialogue in a cultural climate. It speaks for itself.'

'When I discovered that one discipline is not confined to one profession, I discovered everything. When I understood that you're not just a designer or an artist but a *creator*, and that your ideas can be translated and interpreted across many platforms — that's when I started to live.'

'Some of my early designs are now nearly ten years old, and many are still on the market. That feels good. Looking back, I see that my work has evolved, has become a little more settled, more calculated, more comfortable and more human. My first collection, Showtime, was

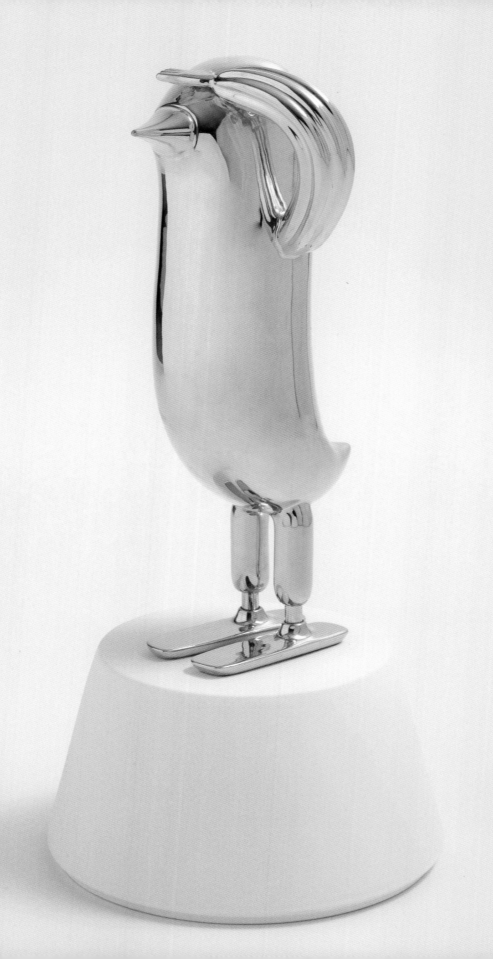

kind of crazy, all gloss and colour, maybe too eclectic. When I work with galleries today, I can focus on something a bit "wilder", but my pieces for the home are more settled.'

'Keeping good energy and integrity in the work – that's what makes me happy. I feel happy in my skin. This is *me*. I'm working, I'm living in the Med, I'm travelling, I have my family, I'm chilling, I still party a little, I'm doing everything. I'm happy, and I believe that feeling comes out in my work.'

'You always make mistakes. I've made plenty. Mistakes are there to be made. There's no glory without mistakes. In every profession and in life.'

'I like to work with materials that come from the earth. I like ceramics, I like textiles, things that are very touchable. In my case, innovation is not about high-tech materials. It's about the thinking that goes into the piece. What is the narrative? What do we want to express? We already know it has to be functional, ecological and well made. But we as designers should give a piece sensitivity and beauty and narrative. The narrative can make it communicate. Objects can make us desire something.'

'Design is a very hard profession. It covers a lot of ground, and you have to be intelligent enough to see the whole picture. You can make a great design, but if it's not photographed well, it won't make it. You can photograph it well, but if you don't have good distribution channels, you're doomed. You can distribute it well, but if you don't publicize it properly, it won't be a success. You also need to understand the DNA of the company that's manufacturing the design. You have to make something sustainable, not just for the earth, but for the company itself. You cannot kill the company you're working for. It's about evolution, not revolution. That is extremely important.'

'There is room for everything. Lots of room. But where is the space for *that* particular piece in today's world? Maybe it's a matter of finding a new combination. Things are still evolving.'

ABOVE **BUBBLE CANDLEHOLDER FOR BOSA, 2012**.

FANTASMICO CLOCK FOR BOSA, 2012.

OPPOSITE PAGE **WITTMANN STAND AT THE SALONE DEL MOBILE, MILAN, ITALY, 2017.**

FOLLOWING SPREAD **HOTEL BARCELÓ TORRE DE MADRID, MADRID, 2017.**

'THERE'S NO GLORY WITHOUT MISTAKES. IN EVERY PROFESSION AND IN LIFE'

'Design has to be for people. You go to a fair and see so much that doesn't work. The chair is uncomfortable or can't be made for an affordable price. It's so boring. Let's get down to earth. People have to *live* with this stuff. That's the thought that drives me and that will move this profession forward.'

'To young designers I say: believe in your work, and work with people you like. Remember that when you do something new, nobody's going to want it at first. People are afraid of what's new. Creativity is about scaring people. It's not about *oooh, it's beautiful, how nice.* It's about doing things you're not sure of, about learning from doing. Evolution is the most important thing for me as a designer.'

KlunderBie

'People are afraid of what's new. Creativity is about scaring people'

Cultural entrepreneur HELLA JONGERIUS has learned to embrace the industry to bring more colour into the world

WORDS
Jeroen Junte

PORTRAITS
Daniel Hofer

WHAT I'VE LEARNED

'I have a great need to lose myself in something. Over the last ten years I've focused completely on colour. The more I read and research, the less I know about the subject. I feel like a beginner again, and it feels good. In that sense, colour is a metaphor for life itself. I've also started painting recently. Not with the pretence of a visual artist, but as a way to experience how colours blend and what the properties of certain pigments are. Once I've become fascinated by a subject, I want to understand it to its core. I become incredibly persistent. That's why I only work with a few companies — ones that offer me freedom. Innovation is only possible if there is room for serendipity — coincidence can push you onto a certain path. I didn't name my studio Jongeriuslab on a whim.'

'My first job was as an occupational therapist. The only resemblance to designing is that you work with your hands. It was mostly a way to escape my upbringing, which had limited room for self-discovery. It felt like an enormous relief when I decided to attend the Design Academy instead. I'd finally found my place. The freedom and non-conformism of the art world drew me in. But I instinctively knew that the Design Academy wasn't the right place for me, either. There was too much freedom. I'm more practical. Even back then, I was fascinated by mechanical processes. To not just make one of something, but a whole series of those things at the same time. I wasn't surrounded by much in the way of art and culture as a child. My mother was a patternmaker, so we did have various sewing machines at home. I even had a small one of my own, but I hated it. I thought, *I'm not going to sew while the men design real industrial products.* But at Design Academy Eindhoven, a world of yarn development, weaving and knitting for the industry opened up. That's how I discovered I had a talent for textiles, even though I only started with that years later. And when you follow your talent, you're in a flow.'

'Design Academy Eindhoven, which wasn't even its name at the time, was more vocational then than it is now. I received a traditional education in industrial design. I learned all kinds of manufacturing techniques, such as making ceramic and injection moulds, and weaving

'I DIDN'T BECOME A DESIGNER JUST TO MAKE PRETTY THINGS'

textiles. These days, you're mostly taught how to have an academic attitude. You have to be able to think in concepts and be critical. Personal development is very important of course, but the skills are lagging behind. Students know very well what they *want* nowadays. They just can't *do* it. But for now, almost all products are made by the industry. So if we don't want our world to be shaped by marketers, we have to sit at that table. Otherwise there won't be any space for research, for experiment, for quality. That's why knowledge of industrial processes is essential. I firmly believe that the economic system has to change – and will change. For that reason, economics should be a mandatory course at design schools.'

'Immediately after my graduation, or during really, I was picked up by Droog Design in 1992. That was the turning point in my career. My work coincided with a movement, which enhanced its cultural importance. I was also influenced by Droog Design's way of thinking. I met influential contemporaries like Jurgen Bey and Piet Hein Eek through the brand. And don't forget the publicity. But in the end, working under the Droog flag became too constricting. By then I had my own fascinations about the mix of industry and craftsmanship, whereas Droog moved towards design art, where huge amounts are paid for often senseless statements. That's not my cup of tea. The brand's logical successor was Super Normal, led by Jasper Morrison. Not that I feel much kinship for that, but it is fresh. And at the least it offers an alternative to an out-of-hand production system that continues to pump out new products, each demanding more attention than the next.'

'I'm a real cultural entrepreneur. Because of that, working for a company or a large design studio isn't an option. That's something I gained from my upbringing. My three brothers are also entrepreneurs, just like my father. To successfully lead an independent studio, you have to be entrepreneurial. You need to be able to assess the risks and also have the courage to take them, free up money for experiments and invest time in research. Apart from these business aspects you have to organize and build a network. Direct your staff and be able to bind them to

ABOVE **KLM BOEING 787 DREAMLINER BUSINESS CLASS, 2015.**

FOLLOWING SPREAD **MODELS FOR THE BREATHING COLOUR EXHIBITION IN LONDON SURROUND JONGERIUS IN HER BERLIN STUDIO. VASE PAINTINGS (2009) ARE VISIBLE ON THE WALL.**

you. And maybe the most important thing of all: have the focus to get where you want to go. All things I'm good at and enjoy doing. I don't like *all* of it, though. In particular, having too many employees can be a burden. I know brilliant designers from my time at Droog who never became successful, because they don't have entrepreneurial skills. It's such a shame.'

'After running a studio for ten years, it became apparent that I'd created a building that didn't fit me. Too many employees, too many clients, too much white noise. I could have gone on successfully for years, but that would have just been more of the same. Something wasn't right, I felt it intuitively. And my intuition is spot on, always. I trust it blindly. The solution was distance. Literally. I closed the studio in Rotterdam and left for Berlin, a city unknown to me. I even wanted to work completely alone at first. In hindsight, this move was one of my best decisions. I like that in Berlin, which has no international design scene worth mentioning, I can work in peace. Luckily, several large clients like KLM and Vitra called in at that moment. Here, I created a new structure and now everything fits.'

'Making exhibitions is an irreplaceable part of my design practice. They're a chance to take a step back and reflect on what I'm doing. Even the panic that comes from once again diving, head first, into something without fully understanding the consequences, is cleansing. In 2003, Alice Rawsthorn gave me the chance to create an exhibition at the Design Museum in London. She was the first to have the guts to put me on an international stage. That opened the door to a bigger playing field; I still feel indebted to her. As such, to be back in the Design Museum in London this summer [2017] is a very special feeling. Breathing Colour is the presentation of ten years of colour research. But in fact, it's a pamphlet against colour monotony. We're bound to a colour system in which the industry uses a very limited palette of pigments. Fortunes are spent on research into scratch resistance or lightfastness, but not on the development of layered colour recipes. According to the industry, a colour always has to be the same, whether it's used on textile or shiny metal. A colour also has to look the same in the

'I BELIEVE IN CHANGING COLOURS THAT BREATHE WITH THE LIGHT'

BELOW **EAST RIVER CHAIR FOR VITRA**, 2014.

TILE SIDE TABLE FOR GALERIE KREO, 2017.

FOLLOWING SPREAD **BREATHING COLOUR EXHIBITION IN THE DESIGN MUSEUM, LONDON, 2017.**

middle of the day as it does at dusk. I, on the other hand, believe in changing colours, colours that breathe with the light. There is no market for such unstable colours, says the industry. This is nonsense. With this exhibition, I want to show consumers that there *is* an alternative to the prevalent colour monotony. Just like the food industry that now has to deal with a consumer who wants to know where his meat comes from or what's in his soup. The industry only listens if you hit them in the wallet.'

'Our world suffers from colour anorexia. It's my mission to change that. But I have to admit, during my work for Vitra I discovered how hard it is to introduce new colours. First, the existing colours have to stay available for a minimum of three years, because clients have to be able to replace furniture. This means that you'll have to have two collections in storage for years. Then there are the technical limitations. A paint fabricator has to develop new pigments. Do new pigments mix well with plastic in an injection mould? And how does that coloured plastic compare to the colours of the woollen upholstery or the varnish for the wood? When that's been sorted out, the marketing division enters the picture. How will the colours be communicated? As a designer you're the filter between the consumer and the industry, with an understanding of what is possible and a vision and need for innovation. This process takes years. But big changes always come in small steps.'

'With the pamphlet 'Beyond the New' that I launched during the Milan Design Week 2015 with critic Louise Schouwenburg, I put myself in a vulnerable position. Up to the day before, we were asking ourselves: *should we do this*? But I feel a responsibility to speak my mind. I'm in a position where people listen to me. I didn't become a designer just to make pretty things.'

Marc Eggimann

Deniz Guzel

From his office in Osaka, industrial designer **TOSHIYUKI KITA** — surrounded by chairs, kitchen tools and robots — talks about 'the appetite to accomplish better design'

WORDS
Kanae Hasegawa

PORTRAITS
Hideaki Hamada

'Osaka is now Japan's second largest city, but before World War II it was a rural area with lush vegetation, rice plants, water and forest inhabited by dragonflies and crickets. I often swam with my schoolmates in the river.'

'At home we kept rabbits, chickens, ducks, paddy birds and fish. They were part of the family. My life was fully integrated with nature. My childhood memories implanted the idea in my mind that nature is the most reliable thing in the world.'

'Around the age of 15, cars and electrical appliances started to filter into my life, and the idea of "design" emerged, carrying with it a sense of the future. As a teenager, the thought of becoming a designer felt like an opportunity to enter the near future one step ahead of everyone else. After graduating from university, I started to work for an aluminium company.'

'The Saruyama sofa went on the market in 1971. Moroso still has it in production. It's a funny piece. It recalls a mountainous landscape while inviting people to sit in an informal way.'

'You have to accept the fact that you'll never be totally satisfied with a design. There will always be a feeling that you could have done better or more. But it's this very feeling that has motivated me for over 40 years now.'

'Many things go into making a good design — function, safety, economic viability, environmental impact. A designer has to orchestrate all these aspects to achieve a tactile balance. The ultimate goal of design is to make the user happier. A designer needs to empathize with the broadest public possible, and that means travelling around, gaining a genuine understanding of different cultures and ways of living.'

'If he wants his design to succeed in the market, a designer should direct and manage the entire project, including the advertising and marketing strategy of his product design. It's crucial to become almost a family

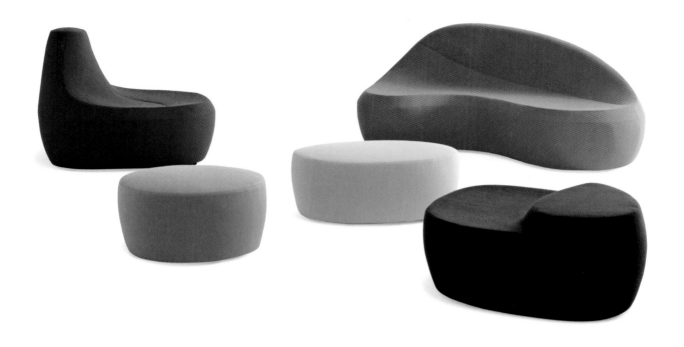

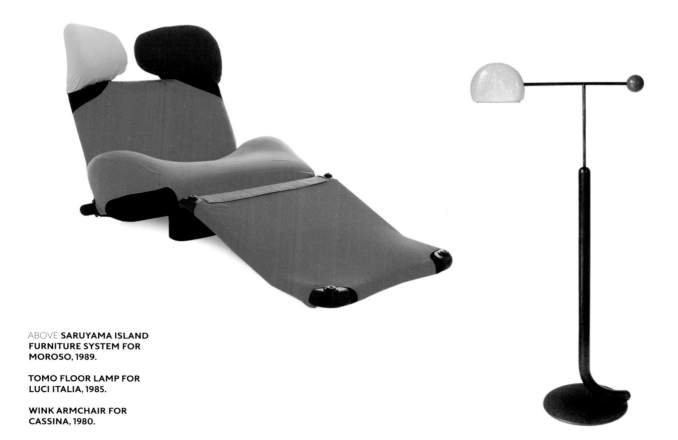

ABOVE **SARUYAMA ISLAND FURNITURE SYSTEM FOR MOROSO, 1989.**

TOMO FLOOR LAMP FOR LUCI ITALIA, 1985.

WINK ARMCHAIR FOR CASSINA, 1980.

ABOVE **AQUOS LCD TV FOR SHARP, 2001.**

OPPOSITE PAGE **KITA'S CAREER STARTED IN 1966 WITH AN ALUMINIUM KETTLE. HIS T CHAIR SERIES FOR ITALIAN FURNITURE BRAND FUTURA WAS LAUNCHED IN 2014.**

BELOW **K06 AKI, BIKI AND CANTA SWIVEL ARMCHAIRS FOR CASSINA, 2000.**

member of the company that manufactures your work. When I designed the Aquos LCD TV for Sharp in 2001, I insisted on directing all advertising in order to communicate the brand identity correctly. The freelance designer who wants to build that sort of relationship needs to have someone in the company who's on his side.'

'I always compare the role of the designer to that of a chef. Both create something from available resources, and the reason behind it is to make people happy.'

'Design doesn't come after you've ruminated about it or mulled it over. It comes like a flash.'

'I would like to design for the elderly, to make things that empower older people. And as the car industry enters a new phase, I'm excited about developing new automotive concepts. Other than safe and comfortable transport, what emotional experiences can a car offer?'

KENGO KUMA has learned to nurture his relationship with craftsmen. 'They have taught me how sustainable local materials are'

WORDS
Kanae Hasegawa

PORTRAITS
Tada (Yukai)

KENGO KUMA

'While I was a student at the University of Tokyo in the late 1970s, I worked part time for my teacher, architect Hiroshi Hara. I can remember that period vividly — staying in his office overnight for days at a time, making maquettes. When I saw an established architect like Hiroshi Hara working overnight, I had to do the same. It was an eye-opening experience. I did not know a famous architect would work through the night.'

'Hara told me that you can become an architect if you stay close to an architect. What he meant was that by spending your days and nights with an architect, you realize that he is like any other human being — an ordinary person. People think architecture is a special profession. But once you discover an architect is just like you or me, you feel as if you can become one, too.'

'At one point I was able to accompany my teacher to the Sahara for a two-month expedition. Imagine: just the two of us together, day and night, for 60 days. I got to know Hara as a person. As an architecture student, I saw it as such a precious experience, and a privilege, to have an architect all to myself. As I listened to his views on life, I began to think that I, too, could become an architect.'

'After working for several years at one of the biggest construction companies in the industry, I studied at Columbia University in New York City as a visiting scholar. The approach to architecture there was very different from that of Japan. Architects in Japan are expected to be good draughtsmen who can draw lines. But at Columbia, being a good architect was based on the ability to convincingly articulate ideas.'

'As someone who returned from the States with no realized projects, I found it difficult to get a commission in Japan. I started with a modest project in a small town, Yusuhara, which is in Kōchi Prefecture in southwest Japan. The mayor there asked me to design a small public restroom. I had no work at the time, so I was thrilled and immediately agreed. Then in 1994 the mayor again approached me to do a larger project in the same region: the Kumo-no-Ue-no Hotel.'

ABOVE **ART AND CULTURE CENTRE, BESANÇON, FRANCE, 2013.**

OPPOSITE PAGE **AS A STUDENT, KUMA INTERVIEWED IAN SCHRAGER. NOW THE ARCHITECT IS WORKING ON THE ENTREPRENEUR'S EDITION HOTEL IN TOKYO, WHICH IS EXPECTED TO OPEN IN 2020.**

FOLLOWING SPREAD **PROSTHO MUSEUM RESEARCH CENTRE, AICHI, JAPAN, 2010.**

'I always treasure meeting people. Architecture is the result of mutual trust, and it takes time to build belief among people. During the recession in the early 1990s, it was difficult for architectural projects to be realized in Japan. Young architects had no work. Occasionally, I would get a small project in the remote countryside. I had no choice. But since I had plenty of time, I spent many hours with local carpenters, stone-carvers and other craftsmen who shared their know-how with me. We ate together, and they talked about the local way of living. They taught me how materials from the area — wood, bamboo, paper — are traditionally used in Japanese buildings, and proved how sustainable they are. Through spending so much time together, working on a project, I became very close with the craftsmen and nurtured trust. I respect the skills of craftspeople, and they in turn trust me. Their skills give me hints on how to infuse craftsmanship into a project.'

'I listen to clients, of course. And in the case of public buildings, I listen to the citizens who will use the building in the future. Gaining trust from the public is very important, which is why I try to be on site when there is a public hearing on a project — wherever it may be.'

'Architecture students believe that realizing aspirational projects stems from visionary ideas. No. Grand projects do not *suddenly* materialize from grand ideas. I always tell my students that it is more important to build mutual trust between people.'

'I am still not satisfied with what I do. When I finish a project, I believe I have done my job. But as the years pass, I think of things that I could have done better — small aspects that I could have taken into consideration. Then, as I move to the next project, this feeling of a lack of accomplishment subsides. I always learn from my past. I determine the lesson and incorporate it into my next project. Together, my works are a progression of finding mistakes and making improvements. I have now worked on five projects in the town of Yusuhara, and I am not satisfied with any of them. But in the end, an architect needs to be hungry — to feel unsatisfied — in order to find motivation and move forward.'

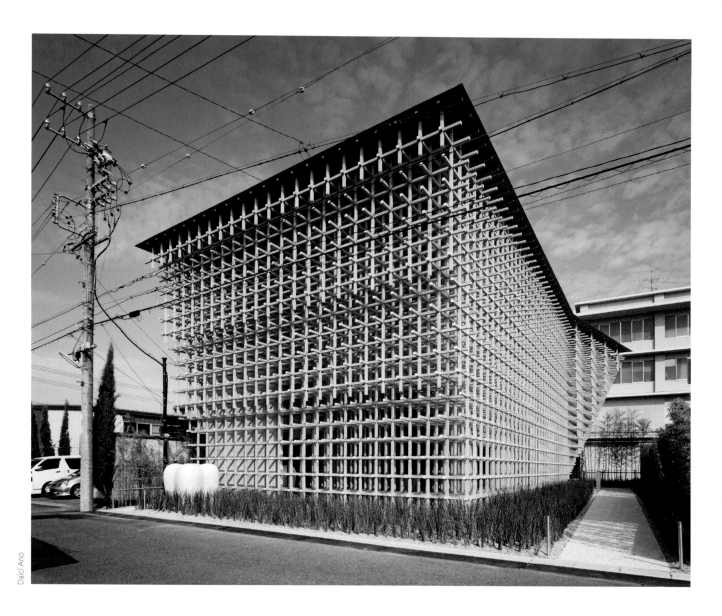

Daici Ano

'Grand projects do not suddenly materialize from grand ideas'

ABOVE AND OPPOSITE PAGE
YUSUHARA MARKET, YUSUHARA, KŌCHI, JAPAN, 2010.

'Until the 1980s, architecture symbolized the Japanese economy and its culture. But after the recession, the people of Japan viewed the discipline as something destructive — a useless way to spend our taxes. People thought we did not need any new buildings. This caused an architectural setback after the '90s. As a result, architects and city planners learned that buildings need to engage society.'

'It is not that I deny flamboyant architecture. I very much admire Ian Schrager, for instance. One of my assignments while studying at Columbia University was to interview the hotelier and submit a report. It was the first time I had interviewed anyone, and I was struck by his energy and his belief in what design can offer to a hospitality environment. He taught me that design can be emotive.'

'I try to make architecture that speaks to people. I like to use Japanese expressions that apply to tactility — *fuwa fuwa*, which translates as "airy", or *zara zara*, meaning "rough" — phrases that are subject to individual interpretation. Maybe what I learned from Schrager has influenced my approach. Funnily enough, I just started working on his new Edition Hotel, which will be built in Tokyo.'

'When designing a building, I do not focus on the overall silhouette but on what each detail conveys. A single project is made up of many details, and I want each specific element to have a voice. I hope people who look at one of my projects can feel what I've tried to do. Historically, architecture was about reading detail. It was more about ornament than decoration. There was meaning behind it.'

'I am very grateful to be working as an authorized licensed architect in France, thanks to permission granted by the École Spéciale d'Architecture. I already had an office in Paris, but a foreign architecture firm that practises in France needs to partner with a local architect. With ESA's authorization, my office can work alone, and that makes a huge difference. I can communicate directly with French engineers and craftspeople.

'ARCHITECTS IN JAPAN ARE EXPECTED TO BE GOOD DRAUGHTSMEN WHO CAN DRAW LINES'

It is more difficult in the US, where each state has its own licensing system. If I want to work on my own in New York, Florida or California, I need licences from all three states. Even though there are US clients who appreciate the essence of Japanese architecture and would like to commission a project, the country's licensing system forms a barrier.'

'My dream for the future is to complete a religious building of some kind – *any* kind. I think that religious architecture can touch the hearts of children who don't know anything about my industry. I have a strong childhood memory of going into a Protestant church that was near my kindergarten. I was mesmerized by the architecture. When I went to my relative's funeral in a temple, I was awestruck by the atmosphere of the place. I cannot explain why, but those buildings simply left a lasting impression on me.'

Satoshi Asakawa

A lover of cities in general and New York in particular, **DANIEL LIBESKIND** shares his thoughts on democracy, gentrification and the art of living together

WORDS
Leo Gullbring

PORTRAITS
Carmen Chan

DANIEL LIBESKIND

1946
Born in Łódź, Poland

1970
Receives degree in architecture at Cooper Union

1987
Wins the final IBA (Internationale Bauausstellung) in Berlin

1989
Wins an international competition for the Jewish Museum (350,000 people toured the building during the two years before its official inauguration in September 2001)

1999
Completes his first building, the Felix Nussbaum Haus, Osnabrück, Germany

2001
Designs the Serpentine Gallery, London

2003
Wins the site plan for Ground Zero
Larry Silverstein, the site's leaseholder, hires David Childs of SOM to design the Freedom Tower

2004
Appointed as the first Cultural Ambassador for Architecture by the US Department of State

2017
Inaugurates Canada's first Holocaust Monument in Ottawa

'Do you know the Shakespeare sonnet that begins like this?

No! Time, thou shalt not boast that I do change.
Thy pyramids built up with newer might
To me are nothing novel, nothing strange;
They are but dressings of a former sight.

It speaks to me. My approach to architectural design hasn't changed over the years. I'm lucky that I do what I love to do, and it doesn't even feel like work. No-one tells me what to do, and I'm in charge of my own time. Creativity means that you work with amazing people: you travel, you meet new faces and you invent things. How lucky can you be? Part of my good luck is that I work with my wife. We are like Yin and Yang. I'd never be an architect if she were not my partner; she does all the things that I'm not able to do.'

'The Jewish Museum was really my first building. I had never designed and built a building before. I was a paper architect at the time, like so many colleagues who are now famous. Half of my life I did things that — according to some people — weren't architecture, but with time I had the chance to balance theory with actual building. Architecture is more than just walls, windows and technology. It's a civic art that feeds on a kind of madness. It requires passion and intensity, and it provokes controversy and differing opinions.'

'It might seem strange that I started my career as an accordion player, but I did. I grew up in Łódź, Poland, in the 1950s, the dark era of Communist repression. I wanted to play the piano as a child, but my parents were scared to have one in the house because of our neighbours, who didn't take kindly to Jews. My accordion came in a suitcase. I became a virtuoso; I actually played on one of the first Polish TV shows. We moved to Israel when I was II. I once joined a music competition with hundreds of other people, including violinists, cellists and flautists. My father carried that heavy suitcase into the room. The jury smiled when they saw the accordion, but stopped smiling when I played Bach's first toccata in D minor. [Violinist and conductor] Isaac Stern laid his

arm around my shoulders and said: "Daniel, you have already exhausted all the possibilities of this instrument. You have to play the piano." But it's very hard to move from playing vertically to horizontally, so I changed my instrument into architecture, and I ended up in a profession that is all about the vertical.'

'My mother truly hated the notion of having to conform to a collective idea, so after two years we left Israel and moved to New York City. My father got a job in a printing shop in downtown New York; my mother became a seamstress in the Bronx, the working-class neighbourhood where our family lived. I studied at the Bronx High School of Science, which has produced more Nobel Prize winners than any secondary school in the world. After graduation, many of my classmates went straight to PhD programmes. I looked for a tuition-free school and applied to Cooper Union, where John Hejduk was the dean.'

'In the past, I was disappointed in contemporary architecture's lack of a humanistic vision. But it's now truly changing, regardless of the tendencies toward totalitarianism you see around the world and in our country. Architects speak a language that communicates with people, and there is a realization that the city is first and foremost for its citizens. Cities are undergoing a kind of renaissance that is slowly permeating the field of building and architecture. It's not just for trained people like engineers and technicians. It's a field for everyone.'

'I learned a lot about how the city works in the making of the master plan for Ground Zero, a project that reaffirmed my deep belief in democracy. You can produce meaningful architecture only through public discourse, controversy and debate, which make for an expression that is true of its time. My plan came under attack from the very beginning, but it pretty much evolved into what my original drawings showed. Ground Zero has given the city a new lease of life. Many people said they would never go downtown again. Now millions of people go there, and I think it will be the new centre of New York for the coming 30 years. Our contribution is attractive for many reasons. First of all, half the site is public space,

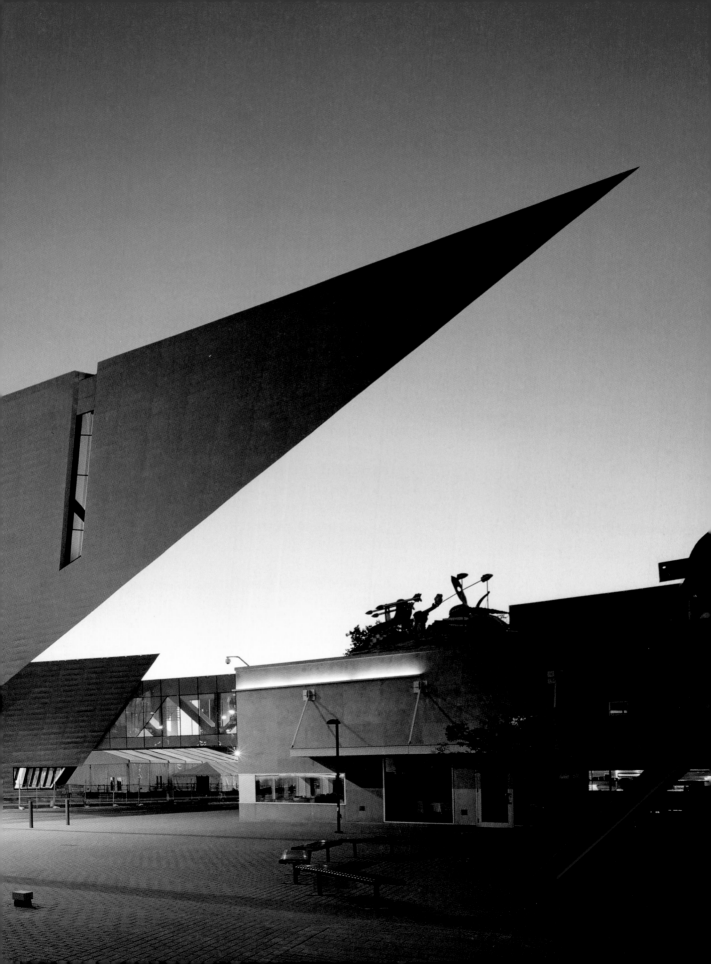

'PEOPLE SHOULD LIVE FREELY WITHOUT BEING CONTROLLED BY MOGULS'

a social aspect that almost none of the great architects in the competition thematized. Secondly, nothing was built on the footprints of the Twin Towers. And thirdly, the buildings are pushed far away from the public space. I asked myself: what will my parents get from this design? They will never go into the tall buildings and the office towers. They will be on the streets, on the subways, on the trains. They will see the buildings from afar. They will get a space that belongs to them.'

'Sure, gentrification is a double-sided thing; it can be used as an urban-renewal tool for good or for bad. I'm working on affordable housing here in New York and in Germany, and I'm convinced that income disparity cannot be sustained. Without looking at the city as a whole, you risk creating gated neighbourhoods. That's why people moved to Brooklyn, which has gotten so expensive that people now go to Queens instead. We should be able to steer things politically towards a more democratic city that allows people to live freely without being controlled by moguls who are not even there. The beauty of New York is that you can go to Williamsburg and see the Hasidic Jews along with the African-Americans. They might not love each other, but they learn how to tolerate each other. This city is made up of a lot of different people with different religions. The global population increase will force people to live together, and that will alter the world. So instead of raising walls, creating enclaves and separating people, we should bring them together. Humans pretty much share the same basic needs all around the world. Access to a dignified, beautiful and true place is a universal ideal of modernism that now appears in a different form. What makes architecture so interesting — and also keeps it from changing rapidly — is that it's based on sediments of memory, which to a large extent reside in the unconsciousness. We can compare the city to the human mind. We all carry layers and layers of invisible history with us, but we have access to only the tip of the iceberg. Memory will become much more important in the future. It's not information that counts — we can get information by googling and clicking — but meaning. The ultimate meaning can't be deduced from information.'

OPPOSITE PAGE **NATIONAL HOLOCAUST MONUMENT, OTTAWA, CANADA, 2017.**

Bitterbredt

'Architecture should be a disturbance, an awakening'

'We have had 4,000 years of linear writing since the time of the Semitic tribes, but it's slowly being substituted by images again. That's why people are moving back to idolatry. My advice to young architects and students is to stay awake and take risks. Don't believe everything that you're being fed, and do realize that your liberty and freedom presuppose that others are free as well. Either we are entering an era of true enlightenment, or it might be the contrary, like in medieval times when only a few people were able to read the books.'

'New tools allow us to be in touch with the whole world. The immateriality of technology sometimes seems enough to bring us happiness. People occasionally ask why we need tangible architecture, when we can get everything through an expanded virtual reality. I'd say the opposite is true. For reality to trigger our senses, architecture is more important than ever. We live in dangerous times. A small elite tries to control the behaviour of people through a few algorithms. Totalitarians and strong men are admired, and anti-Semitism and racism abound. Despite this, I'm very optimistic, but architecture has to be humanistic. Preserving a realm of freedom in the city entails a spatial struggle.'

'Most architects give answers, but I believe that architecture — like philosophy, art, and music — should pose questions. This is at the heart of my deepest Jewish sensibility. Who are we? Why are we here? Where are we going? Architecture should not be about fetishizing objects but about navigating such questions, so we can aspire to a better life. All my buildings, beginning with the Jewish Museum in Berlin, are like books without text. They spatially recast memory. Architecture should be a disturbance, an awakening. As Kafka wrote: "A book must be the axe for the frozen sea within us."'

JOEP VAN LIESHOUT

has produced weapons, alcohol, drugs and abortion clinics. 'I don't have regrets, because I'm blessed with a terrible memory'

WORDS
Jeannette Petrik

PORTRAITS
Marte Visser

JOEP VAN LIESHOUT

1963
Born in Ravenstein,
the Netherlands

1988
Shows first solo exhibition
at Galerie Fons Welters,
Amsterdam

1995
Tours the US for the first
time with Mobile Home,
which is now part of the
Prada collection
Arrested in the name
of art

2001
Establishes AVL-Ville in
the port of Rotterdam, a
free state with its own
constitution, currency
and flag

2010
Exhibits a large body
of work at Rotterdam's
Submarine Wharf
(in collaboration with
Museum Boijmans
Van Beuningen)

2013
Establishes AVL-Mundo,
Van Lieshout's foundation
dedicated to art

2015-17
Shows one of Atelier
Van Lieshout's largest
installations at
Ruhrtriennale, Bochum

OPPOSITE PAGE **DOMESTIKATOR,
CENTRE POMPIDOU, PARIS, 2015.**

PREVIOUS PAGE **'BEHIND THE
PROJECT LIES A VERY ROMANTIC
IDEA ABOUT THE IMPORTANCE
OF LIFE,' SAYS VAN LIESHOUT OF
NEW TRIBAL LABYRINTH. FOOD
PROCESSOR (2015) IS A RECENT
WORK FROM THE SERIES.**

FOLLOWING SPREAD **HUIZE
ORGANUS, ZUIDERZEEMUSEUM,
ENKHUIZEN, 2008.**

'I've always had this idea about starting a revolution — about overthrowing the world. I don't have a political background; I just wanted to start a revolution. I used to be a communist and an anarchist, but that was when I was about 15.'

'My family was middle class, and it was logical for me to become a self-made man like my father. He grew up in very poor conditions and climbed his way up to the middle class. I had to do that too, and I don't regret it. A different upbringing might have helped me to understand certain things faster or to have a different network, but I'm happy with the way things went. It was the hard way, but it's interesting to learn how to do everything yourself.'

'I was extremely young when I started art school. As a 16-year-old from a village, I was a bit of an outsider. Others at the school had done military service or studied before. They'd *lived*. I was often on my own, which was good for me. This was in 1980. It was a time of full-on punk, squatting, crisis and a lot of idealism. There was a very strong left-socialist movement, with demonstrations and the like. Someone I met introduced me to political thought. She was a communist, of course. Everyone was. Apparently it was a cool thing to be.'

'If I hadn't gone to art school, I would probably have studied physics and become an inventor. I like to think about how I can improve things. I'm never satisfied, always thinking that things could be different.'

'Squatting became difficult recently, but I still live in a building that started out as a squat before being legalized. [Van Lieshout's studio is in the same building.] Today I express my thoughts through my work, which is still critical of society. I wouldn't call it political. It's about social criticism.'

'*SlaveCity* portrays a horribly rationalized and hyper-organized society in which Excel sheets dictate life. I'm currently working on *New Tribal Labyrinth* [an ongoing series that began in 2011]. I'm reinventing the Industrial Revolution by really going back to the roots of modern

Jean-Pierre Vaillancourt

'My art speaks about
our society and about
how we organize it'

ABOVE **DAALDEROP, 2017.**

OPPOSITE PAGE **VAN LIESHOUT SHOWS OFF THE IMPRESSIVE DIMENSIONS OF BLAST FURNACE (2013). THE PIECE IS PART OF HIS ONGOING NEW TRIBAL LABYRINTH PROJECT, WHICH HE SAYS 'REFERS TO THE ABUNDANCE OF STUFF IN TODAY'S WORLD'.**

'CONFLICT MAKES ART INTERESTING'

production — to the blast furnace, which was used to make everything from casserole dishes to heavy machinery, but not things like iPhones or the kinds of lifestyle products you might find in *Frame*. This is a strong statement that refers to the abundance of stuff in today's world. Behind the project lies a very romantic idea about the importance of life.'

'In 2001 I created a free state here in the harbour [at Atelier Van Lieshout in Rotterdam]. We do things differently now. We've become bigger and better — and more organized. We bought two buildings next-door to use as an exhibition space and an artist residency programme. We also collaborate with the neighbourhood food garden. We're trying to improve the area on a local and international level through my practice. What I'm really good at is making works of art, so you might say it's a very megalomaniac place. By making art, I communicate my ideas, which speak about our society and about how we organize it. My art makes people think, I hope.'

'To set up the free state, we basically squatted a piece of land and started filling it with housing, restaurants, a workshop for weapons and bombs, an abortion clinic — all kinds of stuff. We built on the squatted land and wanted to be independent. We had a power plant and water-purification systems. We decided to forgo any rules; you could do what you wanted.'

'I didn't see people going crazy and fucking dogs or anything. Some babies were born. Nothing really bad happened; it was more like a party. But I felt as if all I was doing was talking to the press and to lawyers, which I don't like to do. Nine months is quite a long time for an independent state to survive. If you look at the history of utopian states, that's about average.'

'At that time I really wanted to set up a free state. I saw it as a development towards self-sufficiency. It was necessary as a rebellious act. Nowadays I don't feel the desire to express what I did back then, so there's no need to ask for permits. In reality, though, it's far easier to ask for permits than *not* to do so. It's simply a different time now. Back then I was producing weapons, alcohol, drugs,

medicines and abortion clinics. Our abortion clinic has a permit now. We initially made it for Women on Waves, a Dutch organization that used it for a number of years. Now they just send people a pill by post, and the clinic is ours again.'

'Activism is very one-dimensional in my opinion. There's no depth to it. You might say you're against seals being butchered for fur coats, but there's no underlying layer. The statement says nothing about contemporary life. With art you could say that you don't like seals being slaughtered, but you *do* like naked women in fur coats — as a way of pointing to the complexity of things. You can convey different messages and use layers to create something complex. The conflict of meaning, of interest, of ideology — that's what makes art interesting. That's why art is art. I'm not one-dimensional; I'm multidimensional.'

'I might think that what I'm doing will end up perfect, but it never turns out that way. Being an artist is pretty nasty. There's a lot of insecurity and a lot of competition, and it's very hard to survive financially. I'm doing well, but it's still a bitch, you know? The difficulties of being an artist can't be denied, so you better make sure that the process and the work itself are exciting.'

'I would have liked to marry a billionaire — to have unlimited resources so that money would never be an issue. Then I could buy a steamroller, destroy a city and build beautiful high-rises there — or whatever I felt like building. It's important to go through the struggle of course, but this is a company. We need cash to pay our staff their monthly salaries.'

'In reality, I like making things that nobody wants to have, like *Blast Furnace*. That type of piece costs money, but it will never sell. If I had unlimited resources, maybe I'd become lazy. I don't know. I don't have regrets, because I'm blessed with a terrible memory. I even forget the good things, so good or bad — it's as if nothing's ever happened.'

ABOVE **UNTITLED, 1988.**

GITANE, GALERIE FONS WELTERS, 2000.

OPPOSITE PAGE **TECHNOCRAT, MUSEUM BOIJMANS VAN BEUNINGEN, ROTTERDAM, 2005.**

Freedom, discipline, protest and conservatism: a youth full of contrasts taught Italian architect and designer **PIERO LISSONI** to be open to a wide range of creative projects

WORDS
Monica Zerboni

PORTRAITS
Antonio Campanella

PIERO LISSONI

1956
Born in Seregno, Italy

1978
Graduates from the Polytechnic University of Milan with a degree in architecture

1985
Joins Boffi kitchens as art director and designer

1986
Establishes Lissoni Associati in Milan, together with Nicoletta Canesi Later additions include Lissoni Architettura and New York City-based Lissoni Inc.

1996
Sets up GraphX, the graphic-design department of his studio

2006
Presents the book *Liquid Space: 70 Years of Boffi Design*

2010
Designs the Audrey chair for Kartell

2012
Converts Amsterdam's former music conservatory into the Conservatorium Hotel

2014
With GraphX, designs the global corporate identity for Glas Italia

2015
Designs the Fantini showroom in Milan

2016
Realizes the Roomers Hotel in Baden Baden, Germany

OPPOSITE PAGE **ROOMERS HOTEL, BADEN BADEN, GERMANY, 2017.**

'I was born on the outskirts of Milan, in the industrial village of Seregno. My family was marked by interesting personalities – principally my grandfathers, one who was a socialist and an anarchist and the other a communist and an aristocrat. From them I gained a taste for fantasy and an intolerance for rules. My father was a restorer of antique furniture and mostly of old fabrics. He imparted to me a feel for beautiful things but also showed me the *importance* of rules. I grew up between freedom and discipline, and I have certainly taken in something of both worlds.'

'At an early age, I learned how to draw. My father taught me. I wanted to be an architect, although I considered unconventional jobs, too, but nothing like a pilot or a surgeon or a climber. To be honest, at a certain time I was not sure whether I wanted to be an architect or a ski instructor, but eventually common sense prevailed – and my father's opinion, too. Skiing has remained my favourite hobby, though. I must confess that today I make architecture that allows me to have as many ski holidays as possible.'

'I attended the School of Architecture at the Polytechnic University of Milan in the late 1970s, during a time I call the Counter-Reformation. After the years of student protests and political struggles, I found myself in a rigid academic setting with a very conservative view of architecture. But a combination of the rational and the creative made for a stimulating atmosphere. Technical subjects, such as industrial design, as well as the more humanistic ones, like the history of architecture, were approached with a deeply critical spirit. Among my teachers were extraordinary personalities like Achille Castiglioni and Marco Zanuso. With them I learned to see architects as modern humanists. Through their teachings I came to envision architecture and design as one all-inclusive discipline.'

'I have never believed in a specialized way of life. For me, to be an architect means to be flexible. You have to be open and able to make projects that embrace total design. You can change the scale and design of a watch, for instance, to make a building. I enjoy working like a

Federico Cedrone

child, full of curiosity and always eager to play with a new toy.'

'I wasn't one of the better students, not because I lacked enthusiasm but because I studied and worked simultaneously. I learned a lot while practising at a top studio in Milan, where I made many contacts. During those years, I attended summer classes at architecture schools and universities around the world, from New York to London.'

'My professional career began when I became an art director for Boffi kitchens. My first studio was my kitchen at home. In 1986 I opened my first office, along with a partner, Nicoletta Canesi. At the beginning I chose to be an art director and not an architect, because I did not want to accept compromises. At that time Italian architecture was based only on competitions, an ideologically old model, in my opinion. I saw it as a way of selling oneself to the best buyer.'

'The world of industrial design couldn't exist without design companies that challenge themselves and take risks. Even the most notable names in the history of industrial design — Scarpa, Castiglioni, Zanuso, Mario Bellini, the Bouroullec brothers — owe their international reputations to the illuminated policies of good design companies, the strength of their brands and their innovative cultural backgrounds. I feel part of a common creative process with each company that produces my work. There is no sense of interdependence between me and my clients. I do not oblige them to do something, and they do not influence my work. What's important is to be coherently self-contained and to match what I do with the DNA of my client's company. I feel grateful to him for the risk he takes in letting me work for his brand.'

'As a designer, I have no contact with the final user of the products I make. I can only guess who he is from the company's story. When I draw, I never try to meet the needs of a potential customer, because I don't know him.'

'To work as a graphic designer, to create an object or to plan a building, you need different levels of sensibility. If

FOLLOWING SPREAD
CONSERVATORIUM HOTEL, AMSTERDAM, NETHERLANDS, 2012.

BELOW **UPON OPENING HIS FIRST STUDIO, PIERO LISSONI CHOSE TO BE AN ART DIRECTOR INSTEAD OF AN ARCHITECT, BECAUSE HE DIDN'T WANT TO ACCEPT THE COMPROMISES COMMON IN ITALY'S COMPETITION-BASED ARCHITECTURE PRACTICE AT THAT TIME.**

'I MAKE ARCHITEC- TURE THAT ALLOWS ME TO HAVE AS MANY SKI HOLIDAYS AS POSSIBLE'

you are a graphic designer like the ones in our studio — specializing in institutional communication, packaging or corporate identity rather than in advertising — the damage you can do to the company you represent is a venial sin. The object you make must be as pure and clear as crystal. If you mess up, your error is not harmless but also not irreparable. Perhaps your client won't give you a second chance and customers won't buy an object you designed any more. By contrast, your responsibility is frightening when it comes to architecture. In that case, your mistake affects not only your client but a whole community of people, for many years to come.'

'I really like making architecture, not to boost my ego or to leave my signature on the world, but for the thrill of the overall process. When I design a building, I find it impossible to think only about the shell and to leave the technical parts and the interior architecture to others. I am convinced that architecture has to interact with the interior, the environment and the human beings. I do not accept the idea of disconnecting the different aspects of my work.'

'I like making buildings that last for 25 or 30 years, using materials that are fully recyclable after that time has expired. Today's architecture projects should be ener- gy-efficient. They should not use more energy than they require. I'm talking about zero-energy buildings. As an old anarchist, I consider further discussion on sustain- able architecture a worn-out mantra.'

'Among the objects I've designed during my long career, the bad ones are my favourites, because I try to learn from my mistakes so that I won't make them again.'

'The ideal product should reveal the idea and the research behind it — and have a certain amount of style. A long period of reflection goes into a design project. The development phase can take years of deliberation and constant modification. I normally work on small- scale prototypes before making a 1:1 scale unit. Eventu- ally I start to remodel the object — a bit thinner here, a bit thicker there — and the work becomes a project.'

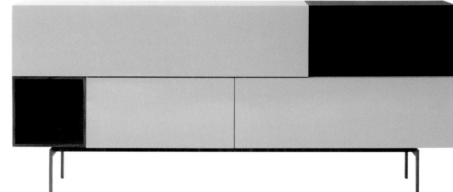

ABOVE **MOSAIQUE SOFA FOR DE PADOVA, 2017.**

MATERIC TABLE FOR PORRO, 2017.

PIOGGIA DINING CHAIR FOR PORRO, 2017.

FROG CHAIR FOR LIVING DIVANI, 1995-2015.

MODERN DRESSER FOR PORRO, 2017.

'THERE IS NO SENSE OF INTERDE-PENDENCE BETWEEN ME AND MY CLIENTS'

'Our Milan studio has a staff of 70, half of which are foreigners from all over the world. The atmosphere has a positive vibe, thanks to their different experiences and sensibilities. Our official working language is English.'

'One department of the studio is GraphX, which I founded 20 years ago when graphics was becoming an increasingly important part of our work. Although GraphX features a team of graphic designers, other kinds of designers may also be involved, depending on the type of project. All in all, the company is made up of flexible players with complementary skills. Groups vary according to the kind of commission, and everyone has an opportunity to interact and to participate in new experiences.'

'Sometimes I work with my son, Francesco, on unique pieces. I like the production side, but I'm not as good at it as he is.'

'In my eyes, design means industrial design. Without the industrial aspect, the result isn't as impressive.'

'Even though I usually develop an idea by myself, I do share my visions with my partners. Our studio is filled with energy. Discussions can be extremely passionate, but I never try to impose my ideas just because I'm the boss. I accept the opinions of my staff, and we discuss them together.'

'Good design needs collective thought. I never step out of the shower in the morning with a winning idea.'

Ten years in a boarding school taught **ELLEN VAN LOON** how to create a private space in her mind — a skill that serves her well as OMA partner

WORDS
David Keuning

PORTRAITS
Floor Knaapen

WHAT I'VE LEARNED

'I grew up on the water. I lived in a barge for the first seven years of my life. My parents transported freight between Rotterdam and other European ports – like Basel, for instance. As a child, I spent a lot of time in and around harbour areas. I know the port of Rotterdam like the back of my hand. Its harsh atmosphere made an enormous impression on me as a child. That port is *so* huge. If you set off seawards from Rotterdam, through Europoort, you pass ocean-going vessels whose steel sides rise straight into the air, some 20 or 30 m from the water line. The port was our playground. We sailed to uninhabited islands with our toy boats. That was our life.'

'In the Netherlands, bargees' children go to boarding school at the age of seven, and I was no exception. I attended a boarding school in Rotterdam until I was 17. There are relatively few Dutch boarding schools, especially in comparison with England, where they're much more common. I'm currently working on the design of a private school in Brighton. I understand how the children will live together there.'

'As a child of seven, it was emotionally difficult to live away from my parents, but children are relatively flexible. You make the most of your circumstances. It's that simple. I learned a lot at that school, partly owing to the lack of privacy. Eight to ten children slept in one dormitory room. A clothes closet was the only place I could call my own. As a result, I don't need much privacy now. I have my own room here at the office, but I'm hardly ever there. I'd rather be in the studio, surrounded by my colleagues. Noise never bothers me. As a girl, I learned to create a private space in my mind, no matter where I was. Privacy is my self-made mental sanctuary.'

'When I was little, I was always tinkering, sewing, sketching. I liked to design clothes and to turn my mother's interior upside down. At first I wanted to go to the art academy, but at school I was drawn to the more technical subjects. My favourite was maths. In the end, I chose architecture, which is technical *and* creative. I was interested in the complexity that goes with the combination of the two variables, but I might just as easily have picked another discipline – industrial design or fashion

'DUTCH LIFE WAS LIKE BEING SQUEEZED INTO A CORSET; EVERYONE HAD TO BEHAVE ACCORDING TO THE SAME STANDARDS'

design would have been equally exciting. A creative spirit can go in all sorts of directions.'

'In 1991 I graduated from the Delft University of Technology. I worked in the Netherlands for a short while, but it was horrible. The country felt so small, and Dutch life was like being squeezed into a corset. Everyone had to behave according to the same standards. There was little room for experimentation. I wanted out.'

'London attracted me the most, but my graduation coincided with a major economic downturn in the UK. During that time, most of London's architects were getting by on what they could earn as waiters. Jobs in architecture were nonexistent. Ultimately, my destination was Berlin, which had just undergone a turning point: what Germans call the *Wende*. Germany's reunification afforded architects an intriguing playground, so we all went to Berlin. It was the only place in Europe with work for architects.'

'I left for Berlin without having a job waiting for me. I packed three bags and just took off. To begin with, I worked for a local firm on a building for a private bank with much too much money. The project proved to be good for me at the time. I then had a short stint at Léon Wohlhage, a company associated with modern architecture, which was right up my alley. I stayed in Berlin and joined Foster and Partners, where I worked for six years on the Reichstag.'

'I'd always wanted to work with Foster, not because I was a big fan of his architecture but because he ran the most well-oiled, most professional machine imaginable. He didn't hide his success under a barrel — not then and not now. I was eager to see it with my own eyes. I had planned to stay only a year or so, but being engrossed in such a fascinating project, I wanted to persevere. It was an interesting experience that taught me the best way for a big architecture firm made up of diverse teams to organize a process that yields a good product.'

'Before the Reichstag was completed, I was both pregnant and homesick for the Netherlands. Don't ask me

CASA DA MÚSICA CONCERT HALL,
PORTO, PORTUGAL, 1999-2005.

Philippe Ruault

why, but going back was a deep desire. When you're pregnant, you make emotional decisions that are not necessarily rational.'

'Initially, as a student, I wasn't overly impressed by Rem and his work, but when he gave a talk about his competition design for the library in Paris, I was blown away by the conceptual approach. The effect of his speech stayed with me. Even so, I'm glad I didn't join OMA immediately after graduation. The experience I gathered before arriving here probably made it easier for me than for people who come straight from university.'

'I prefer to work on very big projects. Small buildings are not really my thing. The more complex, the more interesting. The design of a large project can't be understood all at once. I see it as an advantage, because the sheer size forces you to consider the separate layers of the architecture over a longer period. Big projects give you the time needed to develop the various layers, independent of one another.'

'In the case of Rijnstraat 8, a building that houses a number of Dutch ministries, our redesign went beyond offices and workstations to include representation and the political process. The same can be said of the building for the Dutch House of Commons, which OMA will renovate in the near future. What exactly happens in the political process and where does it take place? And how do people meet one another? Our client − the government − talks about "formal" and "informal" methods of working, terms that imply all sorts of intermediate layers that aren't expressed in words because they're not politically correct. That leads me to the roles of lobbyists and journalists, among others, who are also involved in the political process. As an architect, you want to enable such roles spatially while also expressing them architecturally. The theatricality of politics, which is obvious in countries like France and Italy, is something the Dutch would rather not contemplate. In England, many political decisions are taken in clubs, in environments that are reminiscent of classic cigar salons. It's all theatre, and I like to use the same tactics in some of our Dutch projects.'

ABOVE 'INITIALLY, AS A STUDENT, I WASN'T OVERLY IMPRESSED BY REM AND HIS WORK,' SAYS ELLEN VAN LOON.

OPPOSITE PAGE DE ROTTERDAM OFFICES, APARTMENTS, AND HOTEL, ROTTERDAM, NETHERLANDS, 1997-2013.

FOLLOWING SPREAD RIJNSTRAAT GOVERNMENT OFFICE BUILDING, THE HAGUE, NETHERLANDS, 2012-17.

'The Rothschild Bank in London is a fantastic case in point. The Rothschilds are a Jewish family, originally German, with an enormous history and an enormous archive. Tradition within the organization is quite explicit, but it doesn't appear on paper. It took me two years to understand how it worked. A good example would be the renderings we made for the planning application, which included Photoshopped figures – a couple of bearded men among them. The first comment I heard was: "At Rothschild, nobody has a beard." It's an unwritten law that the entire staff is aware of. "No hats either. Remove them as well."'

'Social processes within a building have consequences for the architecture. In their former office, for instance, they had directors' dining rooms, where the executives had lunch. Very traditional. Every day at noon, a couple of people from the organization are invited to join them. Receiving an invitation means being recognized for an outstanding achievement. I find that terribly interesting. Banks like Rothschilds are extremely conservative organizations, and these bankers were accustomed to classic rooms, with wooden wainscoting, old masters and antique furniture. We wanted to make a modern interpretation of their familiar surroundings – to do something with their history, but not literally. It took buckets of blood, sweat and tears to convince them. You not only have to research an organization's history; you also have to persuade your client to follow the direction you have in mind. These are intensive processes. Most people resist change.'

'The most important lesson I learned from all these projects is: don't take anything for granted. Make sure to question customs and traditions. Be sceptical about everything you encounter and always stop to reconsider. Doing these things makes every project an adventure. And don't be afraid of a challenge. I'm certainly not. We can fly to the moon and back, and anything's possible in architecture.'

'A CREATIVE SPIRIT CAN GO IN ALL SORTS OF DIRECTIONS'

Without complacency, INGO MAURER continues to put out new work well into his eighties. 'When I do something new, I still feel insecure'

WORDS
Tim Groen

PORTRAITS
Elsbeth Struijk van Bergen

INGO MAURER

OPPOSITE PAGE **UNDERGROUND STATION WESTFRIEDHOF, MUNICH, 1998.**

FOLLOWING SPREAD **FLYING FLAMES CHANDELIER IN FRONT OF A REPRODUCTION OF THE LAST SUPPER, SPAZIO KRIZIA, MILAN, 2013.**

'I spent my childhood on an island in Lake Constance, near the Swiss border, where I went through difficult years during the war. I consider myself blessed growing up on an island, because you're surrounded by light. My father was a fisherman, and I spent a lot of time with him on the lake. I saw things dancing in the light, an experience that I applied to my work years later.'

'I think of myself as a weed. I just grew, and a weed always comes back up. I went to school for only six years because of the war. That was *it*. I studied typography for three years and then commercial art in Munich. In 1960 I escaped to the US where – during that first stint – I remained for three years, working for a small advertising agency as graphic designer and art director.'

'In 1966 I designed my first commercial object, Bulb. I was in Venice for a project involving glass. I stayed at a very cheap *penzione*. One day, after having lunch by myself, I went back to my tiny room, a little drunk, and noticed this fantastic 15-watt light bulb. I completely fell in love with it. All I could think was: I have to do something with this. Later I took my sketches to Murano, where they created the glass element, and that was more or less the start.'

'I think the design that's closest to my soul is Don Quixote, a lamp I made in 1989. It combines a lot of different techniques and elements. Commercially, it hasn't been extremely successful, but I think it's one of the most daring lamps I've done. It represents my freedom.'

On an average working day in Munich, I'll come in, say a big hello to everyone and have my espresso – with a splash of Fernet Branca, just to 'kick' my brain. Then we get to work on some 30 different projects, which are running simultaneously. They range from big public projects, like entire subway stations, to unique lights and collection pieces.'

'My development department consists of about 15 people, but the total staff numbers around 70. So that's what we do: come up with pay cheques every month. I feel like I'm playing Risk! [Laughs.] My daughter, Claude, joined

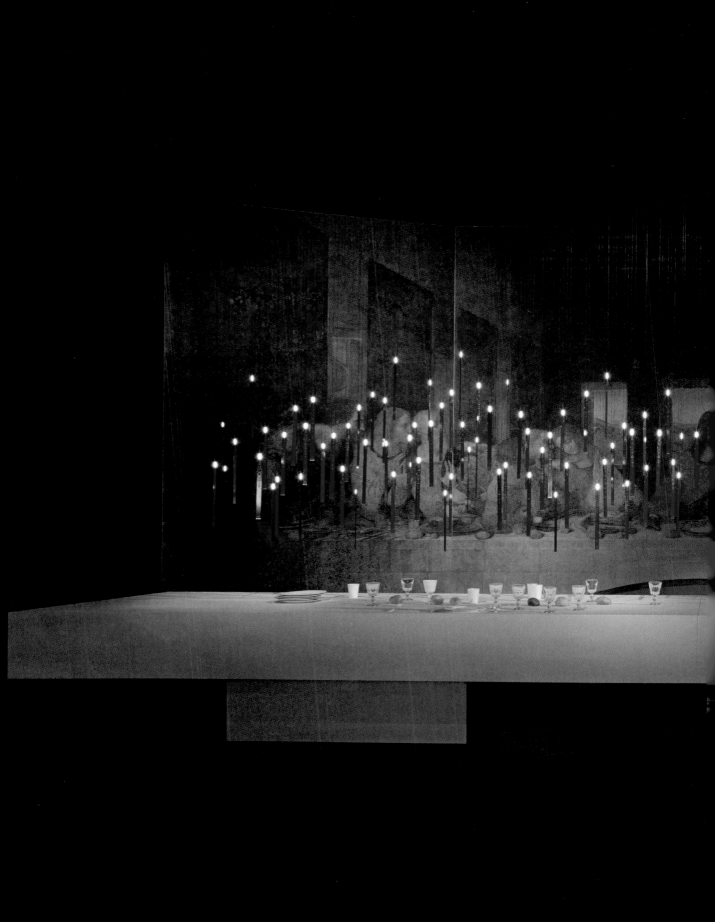

me nine years ago. The two of us face the same problems in our work, but she is very precise, whereas I'm a dreamer.'

'Munich is a super place to produce; it's very well connected. But the city has become extremely rich and has no provocative qualities. In Munich I just work; I have almost no social life there.'

'In New York, I have my place in Tribeca. I've had it since 1997. It was — *we* were — very wild, but things have calmed down. Still, New York is where I get my inspiration. It's also where I have my store [in SoHo], and it's where my best friends live.'

'The younger generation of designers includes some really courageous guys, and I appreciate a number of them. I love their freshness, boldness and naivety. But I'm also confused by their need to start from point zero, when they have so much information at their fingertips and can see how older designers have already been where they are going. I find that ignorant, but maybe it's because when you're young, you're not always certain of what you're doing. Although I must say that the younger generation tends to have a pretty inflated sense of self-esteem, often without reason. [Smiles.] I like it when people doubt themselves and don't mind admitting it. When I do something new, I still feel insecure.'

'A good designer needs to have a lot of passion. It's important to enjoy the entire process, from concept to final product. It's like going on a little trip, with ups and downs, and meeting a lot of people, from technicians to photographers, along the way.'

ABOVE **LUCELLINO TABLE LAMP, 1992.**

DON QUIXOTE, 1989.

OPPOSITE PAGE **MAURER POSING WITH ONE NEW FLAME (2013) IN HIS MUNICH SHOWROOM.**

FOLLOWING SPREAD **ENTRANCE TO THE KRUISHEREN HOTEL, MAASTRICHT, NETHERLANDS, 2005.**

JO NAGASAKA of Schemata Architects reflects on how a lack of real-world training gave him a distinctive edge

WORDS
Kanae Hasegawa

PORTRAITS
Tada (Yukai)

WHAT I'VE LEARNED

WHAT I'VE LEARNED

Takumi Ota

JO NAGASAKA

OPPOSITE PAGE **SAYAMA APARTMENT BUILDING, SAYAMA, SAITAMA, JAPAN, 2008.**

'My first work wasn't architecture; it was furniture. After I graduated from Tokyo University of the Arts with an architecture degree in 1998, a friend I'd had since high school asked me to "make something". He didn't specify more than that. Having just left university, without any experience of real-world design, I was at a loss when it came to a carte blanche assignment. Like a detective, I began probing him for clues. What kind of apartment did he live in? How big was it? How did he use it? During those dialogues with my first client, I came to understand that he wanted storage for everything – from home appliances to clothes. He also needed storage that was transportable, in case he should move house. It was difficult, because there wasn't a specific order to the process, but by studying my client's daily habits I arrived at a solution for making something that would improve his comfort.'

'I didn't intend to open a design firm. But when I started working on my first furniture project – together with a friend from university – we needed a company name and a supplier of business cards. I happened upon a word in a book, "schema", which in Japanese means "space in between". We named ourselves Studio Schema.'

'Another friend from university joined the studio, and we became Schemata Architects. Things were difficult back then. We had no work. We had no connections. Nobody approaches young graduates who haven't completed any physical projects. In Japan, architects typically train for five to ten years in an established firm, harnessing their skills and making contacts in the field before opening their own offices. Architects such as Junya Ishigami, Ryuji Nakamura and Yuko Nagayama – peers and friends from my university years – went on to work under the likes of Kazuyo Sejima and Jun Aoki before starting their own practices. I had been working part time for less than a year when I took the leap, without judiciously thinking about my career. After becoming self-employed – and with no work in sight – I was in serious trouble. Then Yuko Nagayama, who was working at Jun Aoki's atelier at the time, called upon me to help with a residential project at their office. This slowly paved the way for my work.'

'PEOPLE NEED A SENSE OF BELONG-ING TO FEEL CONNECTED TO A SHOP'

'When I was young, I felt rushed and frustrated at seeing my peers realize works and build up their careers while I had no portfolio to speak of. But there are different ways of looking at it. Architects who train at famous firms are faced with being labelled as someone from the Kazuyo Sejima school, or the Jun Aoki school, and are expected to live up to that standard or style. Such expectations put a lot of pressure on young aspiring architects. Since I had no experience in the industry, and no one knew who I was, I wasn't expected to have a certain style. I was free to be radical and progressive.'

'Because I hadn't been influenced by a specific style, I started off by mimicking other architects, always realizing that I was copying the ideas of *other people*. I struggled with not being able to come up with something I felt satisfied with.'

'Renovating the Sayama apartment block in 2008 was a turning point. Until then, I'd viewed architectural design as the creation of something new: from zero to ten. I had a certain image of how a house or interior would be used. But in working on the Sayama Flats, I didn't *create* anything; I *subtracted*. I tore away existing walls and floors − almost brutally − to reveal a fresh look. Maybe because I didn't make anything new, I wasn't obsessed with how the owners would use the space. Nowadays, you see a number of these types of renovations, but back then it changed my entire attitude towards architectural design.'

'One of my first moments of inspiration came when I discovered reggae music as a schoolboy. My cousin took me to an event where people were dancing to a reggae tune. I couldn't understand the English lyrics, but the rhythm was unlike anything I thought of as music. I asked my cousin who the musician was and eventually ended up at a record store, requesting something by Bob Marley. I loved visiting that store. The staff knew so much about reggae and told me things about Bob Marley I would have never known otherwise. Our conversations brought me closer to the man and the music. Sometimes, after a long chat, I'd buy one record. I didn't have much money as a teenager. It wasn't a lot of rev-

OPPOSITE PAGE **DESCENTE BLANC CLOTHING STORE, FUKUOKA, JAPAN, 2015-16.**

Takumi Ota

enue for the store, but I think the staff enjoyed telling stories rather than simply selling merchandise. When people with similar interests gather at a shop, sharing their hobbies, the space becomes like a magnet. A community forms. Maybe people stay for three hours and leave with only one item, but the experience makes them return, time and time again.'

'I think people need a sense of belonging to feel connected to a shop. Personally, I don't like shopping. I'm a bit shy, and I feel awkward choosing clothes while the staff wait for me. There are very few stores I go to, and I go to those because I feel at home. That's why I design retail spaces that make people feel comfortable. Where they can talk to the staff. I want to create environments in which, even if you're alone, you don't *feel* lonely.'

ABOVE AND OPPOSITE PAGE **HANARE HOUSE, ISUMI, CHIBA, JAPAN, 2011.**

FOLLOWING SPREAD **OKOMEYA RICE STORE, TOKYO, JAPAN, 2014.**

LYNDON NERI and ROSSANA HU reflect on how coming of age outside their native China has allowed them to translate design ideas from West to East — and vice versa

WORDS
Penny Craswell

PORTRAITS
Olivier Hero

LYNDON: 'I'm Chinese, although I was raised in the Philippines. I grew up in a very strict Chinese family, and with the expectation that I would do well in business, the sciences or maths. Art was never mentioned, but I loved to draw as a kid. I learned to draw before I could talk.'

'My dad sent me to the USA when I was 15. When I went to college, I enrolled as an art major – all along lying and telling him I was studying engineering. When he came to visit, I panicked. I couldn't switch from art to engineering because the requirements were so different, but I figured architecture was a happy medium that would satisfy my father *and* me. He was pleased, because he thought of architecture as real-estate development, and I let him think that for as long as possible. I'm a strong personality when it comes to doing what I want and making sure I'm happy doing it. I never want to compromise on what I enjoy.'

ROSSANA: 'I'm Chinese, and I grew up in Taiwan. My family moved to the USA when I was finishing elementary school. I was like any other kid, going to school, doing what I was told, showing an interest in a variety of subjects. One thing I never really touched on as a child was visual arts – it was considered a side subject.'

'When I was ready for college, I knew I wanted to go to UC Berkeley, but the question was: which major should I take? I chose architecture because, I thought, it uses both sides of the brain. I started my undergraduate degree at Berkeley without really understanding what architecture is at all. When I was deciding what to do at college, I had a real conversation with Lyndon for the first time. He gave me lots of advice.'

LYNDON: 'I had an ulterior motive. I'm three years older, so when Rossana was going through her options, I was already a junior at UC Berkeley. When she was choosing a college, I knew I didn't want to lose my opportunity and let her go to *another* college and meet *another* man! I made my opinion clear and wooed her with my beautiful drawings – she saw those drawings and believed they were what architecture is about. When she started

studying, though, she quickly realized that architecture isn't just an artistic pursuit.'

ROSSANA: 'We started dating in college. Then Lyndon was off to the Harvard Graduate School of Design while I stayed on the West Coast, finishing at UC Berkeley. After that, I worked in San Francisco while he finished his degree. Then we got married, and I began graduate school at Princeton. Meanwhile, Lyndon worked for several architecture firms in New York before joining Michael Graves.'

LYNDON: 'Later on we worked at Michael Graves together. I was there for ten years, longer than Rossana. We always worked together, even in school; we have complementary skills. We have arguments, obviously, but they're constructive and healthy. We have a lot of respect for each other's ability. In many ways, we need each other. Rossana is "together" in the office and a basket case at home. I'm the opposite.'

ROSSANA: 'We have different ways of looking at things and different architectural talents. We complement each other quite well, whether we're tackling management issues at the office, pursuing a project or working on a design. We're both very conceptual but not in the same way. Lyndon is formalistic and visual, whereas I'm theoretical and historical. At the beginning of a design concept, we brainstorm together. I use words — I like to write things down and research ideas — whereas Lyndon, even at the very beginning, is always drawing. The elements are formed by me talking and him drawing — we act like one person.'

LYNDON: 'Rossana is more logical, and I'm more emotional. Nothing really fazes Rossana. Everything fazes me. In terms of management and organization or thinking through a problem, she's the rock and *I'm* the basket case — constantly coming up with too many ideas, changing my mind and being dissatisfied. I don't know how to stop sometimes.'

'We're fortunate that Shanghai has been our base. When we came here 11 years ago to set up Neri&Hu, this

ABOVE **LANTERN TABLE LIGHT FOR CLASSICON, 2017.**

SHAKER DINING CHAIR FOR NERI&HU (PRODUCED BY DE LA ESPADA), 2015.

FOLLOWING SPREAD **AS NERI&HU, LYNDON NERI AND ROSSANA HU — PARTNERS AT HOME AND AT WORK — CAN BE PROUD OF A PORTFOLIO THAT INCLUDES INTERIORS, PRODUCT DEVELOPMENT, GRAPHIC DESIGN AND ARCHITECTURE. AMONG THEIR COUNTLESS CLIENTS ARE SELFRIDGES, POLTRONA FRAU, OFFECCT, CAMPER AND LE MÉRIDIEN.**

ABOVE AND OPPOSITE PAGE **SUZHOU CHAPEL, SUZHOU, CHINA, 2016.**

town was booming. We were thrust into a place and a time filled with projects that we would never have had the chance to do in the West — interiors, product design, graphic design, architecture: all the things we loved. Some people might have been intimidated by the demand, but Rossana and I were young and foolish. We took it upon ourselves to do something experimental.'

ROSSANA: 'China was a different place back then. We were innocent and idealistic, exploring the issues we were interested in, usually associated with the projects we were asked to do at that time. We were ignorant about how to run an office. We had one purpose — to get the project out there. Now that we're older, we realize why nobody does things the way we did. We managed to survive, though, and we did some interesting work.'

LYNDON: 'We are both Chinese, yet at that time — looking at the country as virtual outsiders — we heard criticism about the Chinese destroying their own cities, copying others and not doing original work. We would go to Milan and people would say, 'You're Chinese, don't take a picture!' It provoked a sense of urgency in us. We thought we had to do something about the situation. Although not yet representing the country we'd left as youngsters, we believed that by doing small things we could start to change some of the perceptions out there. Look at China's past — the Ming Dynasty, for example — and you'll see that lots of beautiful things were produced, but a time came when that stopped. What was important to us was to have a sense of identity as Chinese creatives. That passion drove us, augmented by the boom. Everybody was in a frenzy, and something beautiful emerged from all that chaos.'

ROSSANA: 'When it comes to the projects we do, our exploration of architectural issues deals with themes such as the relationship between public and private, matters of cultural interpretation and memories of things past. We're interested in the history that people live with and in how, in Chinese cities, an entire street can be demolished almost overnight. People's childhoods are being erased. What do we do, as architects, in a city like that?'

'We're a bridge between
different generations
and cultures'

LYNDON: 'It's not an accident that we're in this city. We're fortunate enough to have been given a platform, and we believe God gave us this platform. Our practice has yielded many young practices, and we're happy to see that happening. We started with a passion for showing that Chinese creativity exists. I like to say to those in our generation of architects that we're just bridges. Hopefully, the next generation can use this bridge to get to the next level.'

ROSSANA: 'We're a bridge between different generations and cultures. A big part of our education took place in the West, but the core of our identity is Chinese. We often act as interpreters, not just of the language but of cultural understanding and nuance. We like to unearth what's not obvious. We are architects *and* designers, so we love beautiful things but want the beauty to be a little bit hidden. With our projects, people see more the longer they stay, and each time they return, they find something new.'

After becoming
a father, **LUCA
NICHETTO** changed
his professional
priorities. 'My son
is probably the best
thing I ever designed'

WORDS
Floor Kuitert

PORTRAITS
Antonio Campanella

LUCA NICHETTO

1976
Born in Venice, Italy

1998
Receives degree in industrial design from Università Iuav di Venezia, after studying at the city's Istituto Statale d'Arte

1999
Begins professional career with Murano-based glass-maker Salviati

2000
Designs first product for lighting company Foscarini, marking the start of a long-term collaboration

2001-03
Works for Foscarini as product research and development consultant

2006
Establishes his own practice in Venice

2011
Moves to Stockholm, Sweden, and opens a second studio there

2016
Presents furniture for Casamania, Arflex, Offecct, Verreum and Ethimo at Milan Design Week

'I felt as if I was living like Tom Sawyer when growing up. I was born in Venice but raised on Murano, a super-small island. Because of the water surrounding us, my friends and I would imagine we were pirates. Looking back, I think it was a perfect environment.'

'Murano is known for its glass industry. My grandfather was a glass-blower, my mother a decorator. At least 95 per cent of the people I was connected to in Murano were linked to the glass industry, so creativity was something absolutely normal to me. Probably what I'm doing now is because of being raised amid all that activity. I never *decided* to become a designer. I just went with the flow and started designing glass pieces.'

'My mom was into design. She furnished the house with very interesting products. Our sofa was B&B Italia's Coronado, and our table was the Tulip by Eero Saarinen, in marble. I didn't understand their significance when I was a kid, but I do now.'

'Drawing and history were my favourite classes in primary school. Even before I started school, one thing that really attracted me was the mask of Tutankhamun. My dad had a book about it. I must have read it a thousand times to understand how it was discovered. It helped me to get a feel for beautiful things. I still think that mask is one of the most beautiful objects in the world.'

'I'm not the kind of designer that builds a story after the product is finished, even though the design scene changes and communication has become very important. When I design something, I want it to have a reason — to show why I've done certain things. There is always a story behind those reasons. It could be something very romantic or just pragmatic.'

'As a student, I was very much against people who obligated me to do something that I thought was unnecessary. I know that's not good, but as I think back on my classmates — the very good ones — I see that they are not successful as professionals. On the contrary, some of the bad ones did become successful. I think that's because we have this soul, which pushes and drives us to do what we really want. When you are in school, there is always someone telling you what to do, but the real world is different. No-one tells you what to do. It's *you* that needs to decide.'

'If I could change something in design education, I would close half the schools. There are too many promises made to young designers. Fake promises. We don't need the number of designs that come out each year. That's a big problem, because young people believe that there is space. But it was, and still is, difficult for me. For them, it is a thousand times more difficult. I'm not talking about geniuses, but how many geniuses in one generation do you have?'

'Age is moving in a way. When I was 23, I was probably much more mature than guys that age now. And look at my mom. She was married at 21. In 20 years' time, it will probably be totally fine to start your studies at 25. But when you only enter the market at 30, the time you have to *do* something is short. To do something, you need to build your own career, and to build a career you first need to try things and make mistakes. Talent is not the only thing; it's about experience, knowledge and luck too. University does not tell you this. And you know why? Because I truly believe university is the only money machine in the design industry that is not affected by a financial crisis.'

'People say it's very difficult to understand what the Luca Nichetto style is. I really like that, because I don't want to have one style. To me, style is not design. Design for me means dealing with production, limits and the history of your client's company. Take Castiglioni, for example. Now you look at his products and think — *ah, this is Castiglioni* — because he spent 50 years building a career based on his way of doing things. But he doesn't *have* a style. We *call* that his style. When I'm not here any more and someone mentions "the Luca Nichetto style", it will mean I did a good job, but if my style is recognizable today, it means I'm doing things to boost my ego. It's not my way of thinking about design.'

'You need to be able to match who you are with the DNA

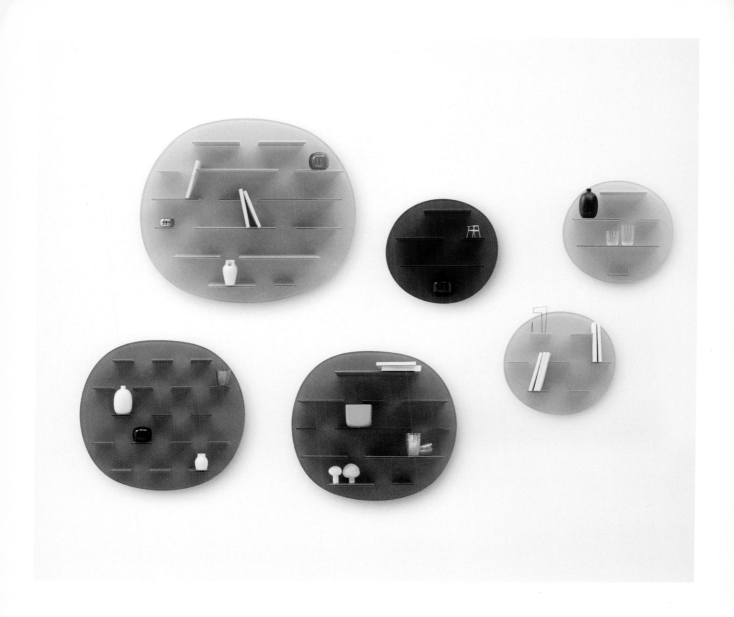

'If my style is recognizable today, it means I'm doing things to boost my ego'

WHAT I'VE LEARNED

of the company. If I were to do the same sort of project for Cassina and Offecct, the results would be totally different. I don't want to be the designer that obliges a company to do something. That way the company disappears, so to speak. It would mean I don't respect them. I'm here to help my clients move on, so the matching part is very important.'

'There is a lot of confusion right now about what design is and what it needs to achieve. There is art design, interaction design and so forth. It's important for "design" to be more than a word. Yes, design should be spread, but what makes it difficult is that there are no more filters, no more boundaries. This complicates design — for me, but especially for young people having to decide what to do.'

'I never go looking for brands, although maybe I should start doing that. I did in the beginning, of course, but currently brands are coming to me. Sometimes I say yes, sometimes no. It's not a matter of big or small, Chinese, Chilean or Italian. The interesting thing is to think what I can do for them and what I can learn from them. If these two things have a positive answer, I will do the project. If I have some doubts, I won't.'

'I learned a lot working for Foscarini. I think my design process is still strongly connected to what I learned there. I was very young, and they pushed me to research material and process, to select samples and to ask for quotations. They taught me about production costs and what they mean to the retailer. I learned more from working than from going to school. Every collaboration is a learning process. That is the beautiful part of being a designer: every project is a new lesson. Good or bad.'

'Language has been the biggest obstacle in my career. Five years ago, I didn't speak English. It's not fantastic now, but I can communicate. I'm not chauvinistic enough to think that design is only in Italy, so one day I told myself that I needed to learn English in order to travel and visit foreign companies. After a while I was able to communicate. That moment opened so many doors for me — it gave me a feeling of freedom, like receiving a driving licence.'

'THERE'S A LOT OF CONFUSION RIGHT NOW ABOUT WHAT DESIGN NEEDS TO ACHIEVE'

'In the last ten years, the production side of design has seen little innovation. The focus shifted from how to *make* a product to how to *sell* a product. Of course 3D printing is an amazing tool, but it's just a tool – that's it. Ten years ago it was carbon fibre that was going to change the industry, but has it, really? It wasn't like polyurethane foam or stretch materials, which completely changed the sofa in the 1950s and '60s. Perhaps the only innovation has been the LED lamp, which changed the shape of lighting completely.'

'My son is probably the best thing I ever designed, but I say that because I became a father only recently. I'm different now and my priorities are different. You need to be very focused, because time becomes shorter and shorter every day. In a way you become more effective, but it's also complicated. I'm travelling a lot, and sometimes I miss a milestone in his life. He says "papa" and I'm in China. It's not something you can get back.'

'The decision to open my own studio was a very practical one. In 2006 – I was still a freelancer – I received a shocking tax bill. I asked my accountant and a lawyer for advice, and they suggested that I buy and open a studio: a tax-wise investment. So I did.'

'Opening a second studio in Sweden was because of love. My wife – then my girlfriend – is Swedish. We met in Venice, where she lived for eight years. She received a very good job offer that meant moving back to Sweden. She's working at an opera house, doing costumes for theatre. At first I travelled back and forth, but it was frustrating, because everything was moving at a fast pace in Italy at that time. In Sweden, I felt as if I was starting all over again. But after a while I started to see it as an opportunity.'

'I advise aspiring designers not to aim for the status of "star designer". Aim for a sector where design can make a difference. There is not a lot of available space, so look at emerging countries with big opportunities, where you can do what is difficult to do in Europe. Many young architects have gone to China, because it's impossible to begin at home. I think it will be the same with design.'

OPPOSITE PAGE **ZAOZUO STORE BEIJING, CHINA, 2016.**

Pondering the life lessons of flea markets, ugly sofas and French snobbery, **INGA SEMPÉ** concludes that patience is a designer's greatest virtue

WORDS
Jill Diane Pope

PORTRAITS
Fiona Torre

INGA SEMPÉ

'I visited flea markets a lot when I was a teenager. I'm very interested in daily life, and a flea market is a strange mix, a summary of many daily lives. I like how everyday things look normal at the time they're made, before their use vanishes and they become extraordinary. I don't like to read books about objects; I don't like to look at pictures. I like to see things in real life — in shops or at flea markets — but not in museums.'

'My parents were very critical about aesthetics. They often said things like *this is awful* and *that is awful*, so early on I became interested in the reasons why people like things. Why do people from certain backgrounds like the same things at the same time? Why are some things fashionable and others not? Also, why do old things look so much smoother and nicer, whereas when they were new they looked shocking?'

'The only modern objects we had at home had a big impact on me. My mother bought everything from flea markets, but she got — and it still surprises me — two new lamps by Vico Magistretti, the small Eclisse ones. I loved to turn them around in my hands. I thought, I *just want to make things like this*. They were so clever. Ever since, I've tried to re-create this particular object, over and over again.'

'I'm totally focused on design. We're surrounded by objects, and I'm constantly looking at them. When I'm waiting for my bags at the airport, I study every piece of luggage that passes in front of me, not because I can't remember which one is mine, but because I'm interested in all of them and in how they are made.'

'I try to design things that will appeal to someone who is 80 as much as to someone who is 20. I don't try to be ultramodern, I don't care about that. I just care about the use of an object; that's the main thing. I think it's important to be outside trends. Otherwise, you rapidly become a caricature. I don't want to make things that are just for one generation. On the contrary, I want to design objects that will be cherished for a long time to come.'

OPPOSITE PAGE **RUBAN MIRRORS FOR HAY, 2015.**

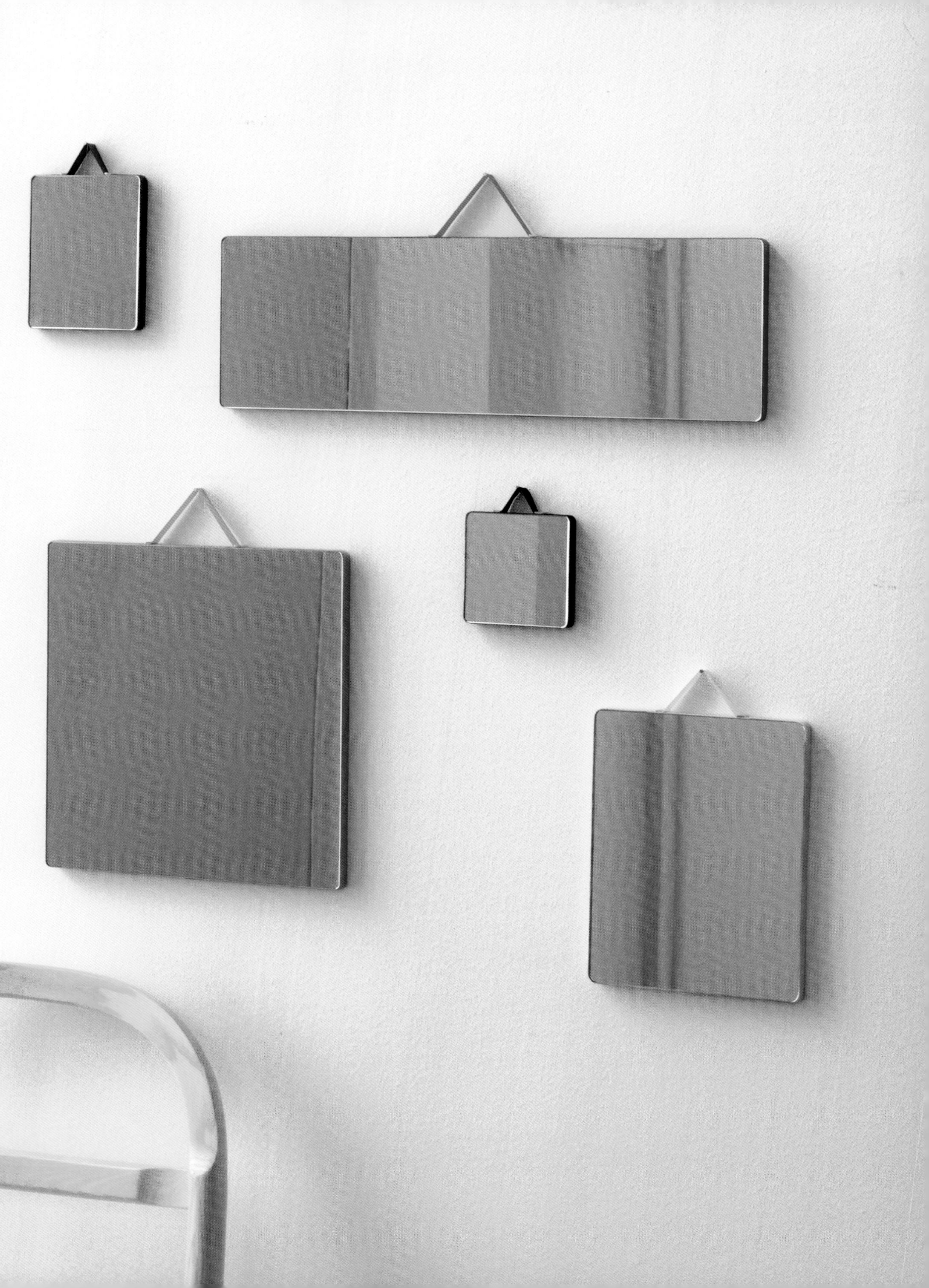
Studio Sempix

'SOFAS ARE CHALLENGING, BECAUSE I ALWAYS WANT TO GIVE UP AT THE FIRST STEP'

'When I was at design school, I had a good feel for objects but no technical knowledge. That side was totally new to me. I learned a lot from the workshops, where we would do mock-ups and make models using real tools — a really important part of my education, because it allowed me to understand the limits that exist in factories. If you just design on a computer, you think there are *no* limits.'

'I try to put my personality into my projects. I don't do projects that I don't like — design is a long process, so why suffer through something you don't find interesting? A project has to seduce me. Choosing the people you work with is very important. Usually I work with family-owned companies for this reason — with people who are deeply involved in their company and its culture, which they want to improve and develop.'

'I always knew that I wanted to be independent. When you say you are starting your own studio, it sounds ridiculous. After all, it's not like you're opening a big office. You're just alone, in your kitchen usually, trying to design something.'

'When I worked with Marc Newson, I learned that you need to know certain processes and techniques from the beginning. Otherwise, you will lose control of the project, and the manufacturer will change it, for good reasons. You have to watch every step. Newson is clever, and he knows processes really well. You might think you finally understand the process, but there is always another way of doing things that you *didn't* know about — or perhaps you thought the project wouldn't be expensive, and it turns out that it is. So I've learned to accept that a project has to change in line with the technical rules involved.'

'The starting point of a project is me making sketches — bad ones, because I'm not interested in doing good, nice-looking sketches. For me, a good sketch is one I can see it in my head and that helps me understand what I want to do. Until that point I keep drawing, and it's very aggravating. Seeing the image in my head is important. That's when I understand myself.'

Rasmus Norlander

ABOVE **PINORAMA PIN BOARD FOR HAY, 2014.**

OPPOSITE PAGE **RUCHÉ COUCH FOR LIGNE ROSET, 2010.**

BEAU FIXE COUCH FOR LIGNE ROSET, 2015.

'I'm more attracted by objects that you manipulate than by furniture, which involves your whole body. Sofas are challenging, because I always want to give up at the first step. The initial prototype is usually awful, and I really don't know how to make it look less like an elephant or less boring. It's hard to find a solution, because the problem isn't technical but aesthetic, and everything rests on my choices. I do like the Ruché sofa that I designed for Ligne Roset Italia, though. It's uncommon, and at the same time it appeals to both young and old.

I like the w153 lamp I did for Wästberg. too. You can clip it onto something or stand it on the table. It's a simple, useful, happy design.'

'It's hard being a designer in France. I'm furious with French politicians who say they are proud of French design, even though we designers don't have any status. I hate the hierarchy of the art world — it's boring, so snobbish. Design in France is associated with manufacturing and the working class; it's not considered a noble profession. Even graphic designers enjoy a special artist's status, which is not given to product designers. That's why I feel a certain contempt for French politics.'

'A designer needs to be patient and tenacious, like a tick. This is important, because you are the one who is fighting — either with or against a company. Your aim is not always the same as theirs, and you have to show them that what you want can also be of interest to them.'

'I think women can be just as misogynistic as men. I've been invited to take part in stories about women designers, whereas there is never a story devoted exclusively to men designers — it's just not logical. If you are a designer and a woman, you are regarded as a woman designer and not just a designer.'

'I don't have big expectations. I don't want to have a big studio. I'm not able to do a lot of projects every year. I like doing things the way I do them now. I would like to work with companies like Leroy Merlin or Carrefour, but the people that run those types of companies are not used to working with designers.'

'Journalists are surprised to hear that I would like to design tools. They think that tools aren't "glamorous", a comment I find completely ridiculous. What's glamorous about designing a sofa? If my designs are sold in the basement of the BHV department store — that's what I call glamour.'

ABOVE **HERRINGBONE GRILL PAN FOR CRANE, 2017.**

OPPOSITE PAGE **INGA SEMPÉ POSES WITH HER LAMPYRE LAMP FOR WÄSTBERG, A ROBUST TAKE ON THE ARCHETYPAL TABLE LAMP IN OPALINE GLASS.**

BERNARD TSCHUMI
talks about his days as a 'paper architect', his experiences with building in New York City, and his dreams for the future

WORDS
Leo Gullbring

PORTRAITS
Andrew Boyle

BERNARD TSCHUMI

1944
Born in Lausanne, Switzerland

1969
Graduates from ETH Zurich after studying in Paris

1976-81
Works on a series of drawings that are published as *The Manhattan Transcripts* in 1981

1982-98
Works on the architecture and urban design of Parc de la Villette in Paris, which was declared a 20th-Century Landmark by the French Minister of Culture in May 2017

1988-2003
Serves as dean of the Graduate School of Architecture, Planning, and Preservation at Columbia University in New York City

2001-09
Designs and builds the Acropolis Museum, Athens

2003-12
Designs and builds the Alésia Museum and Archaeological Park in central France, a complex commemorating the battle between Caesar and the Gauls in 52 BC.

2012
Publishes *Architecture Concepts: Red Is Not a Color*, a retrospective that features Tschumi's insights into architectural theory

'Where did I grow up? I was never in one place. I was born in Lausanne, but my parents lived in Paris as well. I travelled a lot between those two places as a kid, and that's the interesting part of it: one was a small, extremely peaceful, nature-loving town, and the other a big city. The fascination with big cities has never left me.'

'At the age of 17, I found myself here in America as an exchange student. At the time, my interests were geared more towards literature and philosophy, but I was outside my own culture in the States. I spent ten days in Chicago during a Christmas break in 1961. The city was much tougher, rougher and more powerful than it is today. I was on top of one of the tallest buildings in the late afternoon, looking down on the city through the snow-flakes, and I remember it distinctly: the moment I really sensed and discovered the power of the city was like a revelation. I realized I wanted to become an architect.'

'I visited buildings by Louis Sullivan and Frank Lloyd Wright, but it wasn't individual works that fascinated me — it was the encounter with the big city. The 19th-century *Großstadt* of Walter Benjamin, the metropolis, the megalopolis: they represent a fantastic power of culture and intelligence. At the same time, the city can't exist without the countryside. In that respect, Henri Lefebvre's writings are still relevant, although some are more than half a century old. In *The Production of Space* [1974], he combines architectural and urban analysis with political sciences and economics, superimposing situationist ideas on urban space. He uses the example of Tuscany, which at first sight seems like a bucolic, natural landscape, but which has been utterly domesticated by the aristocrats who reside in its cities. It's still important to think about this relationship, but that doesn't necessarily mean that we need to put the village back in the city — I'm thinking of Union Square Greenmarket, just outside our New York office.'

'As a young architect, I was reading what my older colleagues were writing, and I remember being irritated. To me, they were naive, simplistic do-gooders with strange ideologies. Around 1968, an enormous amount of radical questioning took place, to the extent that many existing preconceptions were thrown out. There was this fascination with Italian groups like Archizoom and Superstudio. In a time when you were either political or creative, *they* were both.'

**PARC DE LA VILLETTE, PARIS,
FRANCE, 1982-98.**

'I WON'T CALL IT A MIRACLE, BUT PARC DE LA VILLETTE HAPPENED AT EXACTLY THE RIGHT MOMENT'

'The more established architects at that moment had the idea that we should return to roots and tradition. It was all about contextualism and so on. A number of people were quite exasperated with this regressive attitude. They wanted to continue debating the future of society. I was called a "paper architect", along with young colleagues like Zaha Hadid, Daniel Libeskind, Rem Koolhaas and Wolf Prix. But we were simply trying to use the tools we had at our disposal. In the absence of jobs, we thought a lot about the definition of architecture. Today, I don't hesitate to claim that architecture is the materialization of ideas. You can draw and write about architecture all you want, but you really don't want to end up with nothing more than a series of drawings; they have to be translated into concrete, glass, steel or other materials. Then the material can acquire life and start relating to us humans.'

'*The Manhattan Transcripts* represents the five years I spent on a series of drawings in which I tried to interpret reality architecturally. Those drawings were a tool that gave me an understanding of what I was doing and striving for. It was time to move to the next step, and at almost 40 years of age, I decided to enter a number of competitions that were both anonymous and open to all. The building process was not unknown to me. As a child, I had ventured onto building sites where my father was involved as an architect. But winning the very first competition I entered was a total surprise. It changed everything. I won't call it a miracle, but Parc de la Villette happened at exactly the right moment. I don't think it could have been done before or after.'

'It's true that New York City has gone from erecting second-rate buildings to realizing first-rate architecture. I'd say that until 2001 the city was controlled by a few influential developers and large architecture firms which had been ruling for generations. Breaking into that world seemed impossible. I remember how Richard Rogers tried to build something in Manhattan in the 1980s, but no way – it had to be in New Jersey instead. The discussion about rebuilding downtown after 9/11 showed that the old system couldn't cope politically or architecturally. For better or worse, everything opened up. Previously, it would have been unthinkable for On The Level, a small group of young developers who had never built a freestanding building and didn't know much at all about the architecture scene, to be selected to build the Blue Tower in the Lower East Side. They asked me to design it, after Richard Meier and Robert A. M. Stern had turned them down.'

'We're living in a strange age. On the one hand, it's very fluid and loose. At the same time, the digital culture leaves people craving for materiality. Anything you build now is simultaneously a product of digital technology and a material object. Architecture is facing a huge challenge. Social media and new modes of information transmission are drastically changing the way we live and, with it, the city itself. The situation requires a different approach to architecture. Each generation has thought about the city and has proposed certain models.

ABOVE **BLUE RESIDENTIAL TOWER, NEW YORK, NY, USA, 2004-07.**

OPPOSITE PAGE **BERNARD TSCHUMI WORKED FOR FIVE YEARS ON A SERIES OF DRAWINGS – PUBLISHED IN BOOK FORM AS *THE MANHATTAN TRANSCRIPTS* – BEFORE ENTERING THE PROFESSION AS A PRACTISING ARCHITECT.**

'TO ME, ARCHITECTS WERE NAIVE, SIMPLISTIC DO-GOOD-ERS WITH STRANGE IDEOLOGIES'

The fact that ideologies like modernism, postmodernism, and historicism are now dead has opened the door to creativity. Unfortunately, their replacements have been more about form than about content. Since the '90s, there has been a lack of vision. Architects used to study the history of urbanism, but that's not taught in schools today. Cities are now thought of in terms of transport, property and economic parameters. As a result, no-one is designing cities any more. Urban design is the random outcome of piecemeal decisions, yet never before has so much been built around the world.'

'Our relationship with space has changed completely, because our perception of space has altered. [Russian film director] Sergei Eisenstein claimed in his essay, 'Montage and Architecture' [± 1938], that the Greeks of antiquity invented both architecture and cinematic movement. The idea that architecture isn't static but dynamic is something I worked on during the design of the Acropolis Museum in Athens, where movement through the rooms induces you to experience history. Architecture is a tool for questioning social structures and for exploring the ideas that form those structures. We should not be asked to present solutions but to pose questions.'

'I did urban projects at the beginning of my career, and now I'm impatient to do them again. Climate change is a topic of discussion in the classes I teach at Columbia University, but I want my students to realize that archi-tects — even those who are responsible citizens — are not going to stop climate change simply through archi-tecture. The question of flooding, however, is certainly an architectural issue. I've given my students a problem: what would be the architectural implications if the lower areas of Manhattan were to be flooded by 5 m of water? What would happen if buildings would be sometimes accessible from the land and sometimes from the water? Then I add a twist. The Russian Revolution of 1917 spawned dreams about the future of society. A century later, nobody talks about those dreams any more. How can we access that spirit again today?'

OPPOSITE PAGE **ACROPOLIS MUSEUM, ATHENS, GREECE, 2001-09.**

FOLLOWING SPREAD **ALÉSIA MUSEUM AND ARCHAEOLOGICAL PARK, ALISE-SAINTE-REINE, FRANCE, 2003-12.**

Born in Spain but based in Italy, PATRICIA URQUIOLA is both an architect and a designer. 'I'm a very inclusive person'

WORDS
Floor Kuitert

PORTRAITS
Antonio Campanella

PATRICIA URQUIOLA   223

PATRICIA URQUIOLA

1961
Born in Oviedo, Asturias, Spain

1989
Graduates from the Polytechnic University of Milan after moving to Italy; she first studied architecture at the Polytechnic University of Madrid

1990-92
Serves as assistant lecturer to Achille Castiglioni and Eugenio Bettinelli in Milan and Paris

1990-96
Assumes responsibility for De Padova's new product development office

1996
Becomes head of Lissoni Associati's Design Group and works with Vico Magistretti

1996-2000
Continues working with Piero Lissoni

1998
Enters into partnership with Patrizia Moroso

2001
Opens her own studio in Milan

2015
Is named art director by Italian brand Cassina

'I grew up with a mother who was not always cooking, like many other Italian mammas. She didn't like cooking at all. But in the summer and on weekends we often went to my grandfather's beach house, a half-hour's drive from my birthplace, Oviedo, in the coastal town of Salinas. [Urquiola designed the Salinas kitchen for Boffi.] The house had a big messy kitchen with a table in the middle — not for eating but for working. Whenever you got anywhere near that table, someone would ask for your help. You'd end up cutting bread or cleaning fish. It's the first laboratory I can remember.'

'When I became a designer, my mother said: "How is it possible? You were always breaking down the house!" I was a very curious child, constantly trying to understand things by opening them and taking them apart. She's right — I did break down the house. In the end, there was always a piece left that didn't seem to fit anywhere. Typically a child who's cut out to be a designer, I think.'

'At school, there was a very old workshop where we learned to make things with our hands. I had a very intellectual friend, who now writes for the theatre — she really hated that class, just like another friend who I believe became a lawyer. I used to do all their work. I loved it.'

'When you think of people that work with their hands, it doesn't mean the instrument of thinking is not there. The two are well connected.'

'My mother went to London a lot. I remember her coming back with a necklace made of hair, which she'd seen in a presentation. She also bought fake lashes from Mary Quant. I was ten or 11 when she took me and my cousin with her. We didn't travel very much back then. We went to Liberty, the department store. It was dark inside, with this 1920s atmosphere — fantastic. There was a restaurant on the top floor that was like a rainbow and fitting rooms where you were all together. It's so different now.'

'My mom studied philosophy. She was not the typical mom — our circumstances were different — but she was a fantastic lady. We got a lot of advice from our par-

'EMPATHY IS KEY WHEN WORKING WITH DIFFERENT BRANDS'

ents, who encouraged my three brothers to leave home. "Spain is little. Move! Learn languages, get out of your comfort zone," they would say. I believe in that as well. It makes for a quicker evolution of your personality. It gives you confidence.'

'At a young age I knew I wanted to study architecture. My grandmother's brother was an architect, and two cousins on my mother's side were with architects. It interested me. My brothers and most of my friends didn't know exactly what they were going to do, but I had a clear goal. So I moved to Madrid, because schools in Asturias didn't offer architecture courses.'

'After three years in Madrid, I moved to Italy. Madrid had become too much of a comfort zone. I fell in love and was open to the idea of going somewhere else. In Milan, they didn't validate all the exams I'd passed in Spain. It was a complicated matter, but at that age everything is easy, you know. It wasn't a problem for me.'

'The teachers in Milan, some of whom were architects, were very good designers. One course was called Industrial Design within Architecture, which didn't exist in Madrid. I became both architect and designer. One of my professors was Achille Castiglioni. He taught me to value the tools for living. Thanks to him, I developed a new attitude. Milan was the perfect place for me at that time. Even though the move was complex, in the end it gave me two professions. I was meant to work in both.'

'Architecture and design go together. Things needed for an architecture project sometimes become pieces of design. Six years ago we were doing two hotels at the same time and we needed handles – in fact, we needed *everything*. One job was a resort in America that required outdoor furniture. Right at that moment, B&B Italia wanted to extend its collection to cover outdoor furniture, so I said: "Here I am."'

'The architectural process is not necessarily longer than the design process. That's important to understand. Sometimes it takes longer to put a piece into production or to optimize a new technique than it does to realize an

URQUIOLA BELIEVES IT'S IMPORTANT TO GET OUT OF YOUR COMFORT ZONE, AS 'IT MAKES FOR A QUICKER EVOLUTION OF YOUR PERSONALITY'.

architecture project — at least at the level of architecture that I'm engaged in, which doesn't include the biggest constructions. As a designer, though, I have less distraction and fewer people to deal with. Architecture is complexity. The level of dialogue is much higher because of all the different materials and technical parts. When I'm working as an architect, I often complain and talk about closing the architecture part of my business and keeping only the small design studio.' [She laughs.]

'A designer is a person who faces problems with an open mind — who solves them in a physical way. I need something that makes me begin to work. If you give me a problem, I tackle it with technology. I'm not a visionary; I become visionary because I have to. The input — the problem — amplifies my mind and off I go.'

'Empathy is key when working with different brands. You have to feel and understand the person in front of you, from the inside, even though you arrive from the outside. You have to respect their roots, their heritage — to focus and give it your all. Then you can move from company to company. The dialogue will be different each time. Dealing with different stories works for me. I'm very empathic. I think empathy defines me more than style does. It helps me evolve. I can be in India researching carpets, which are absolutely artisanal, or I can be in Europe working with moulds [for plastic furniture], which are very technical.'

'I'm not a desk person, I often work standing up or sitting on the floor. After one month in the De Padova showroom, my first job, the boss asked me what I wanted to do with my life. I understood that I was being fired, because I was never at my desk. I said I wanted to work in the technical office. The response was *Go!* — and that's where I spent the next six years of my career.'

'Technicians are essential to the process of design. I was lucky enough to learn this while working at De Padova. Metal, wood, fabrics — we used everything. I also learned to respect and even love the firm's very sensible team of technicians.'

ABOVE AND OPPOSITE PAGE **HOTEL IL SERENO, TORNO, ITALY, 2016.**

FOLLOWING SPREAD **HOTEL ROOM MATE GIULIA, MILAN, ITALY, 2014.**

'A designer is a person
who faces problems with
an open mind'

OPPOSITE PAGE 'WOMEN ARE VERY FLEXIBLE, VERY OPEN TO CHANGE,' SAYS PATRICIA URQUIOLA. 'WE PRACTISE BEING ADAPTABLE IN OUR JOBS AS WELL.'

BELOW ARMCHAIR GENDER FOR CASSINA, 2016.

'Working with Piero Lissoni was interesting because he designs for many companies — Cassina, Cappellini and more. Now acquainted with the technical side of design, I learned how to present myself and to relate to each company in a different way. By the time I opened my studio in 2001, I was known as a serious person who liked to work hard, qualities that may have appealed to clients — like Patrizia Moroso, for example, who asked me to do sofas. Collaborating with her boosted my credibility.'

'The first year I ran the studio on my own, but then I met Alberto [Zontone], my husband, and he soon took over the business side of things, giving me the opportunity to spend all my time working on projects.'

'I'm a very inclusive person. My home and my studio are in the same building, because the studio is also part of the family. My daughters find it very natural to live in the same place as my studio. Because everything is connected, I don't waste time. And new ways of working facilitate our lives, of course — not only do family members constantly message one another through WhatsApp. It's also a source of photos pertaining to my projects. I have a chance to approve a design or to make changes, since my team can always communicate with me.'

'I see sensitivity as a democratic quality that is not specifically gender-related. You can't say that men are conceptual and women are sensitive, at least not in my experience. My mother was the more conceptual side of the family and my father, who was an engineer, the more sensitive side. Women are very flexible, very open to change. Women know that if something happens in the family, with the children for example, they have to manage. We practise being adaptable in our jobs as well. That's not a bad thing. We are not insecure about switching points of view or rethinking prejudices.'

'Thinking in terms of goals is a very masculine thing. When I have goals, I keep them quiet. My philosophy is to go step by step and to let things come to me. It's more serene that way. I don't believe in saying that I'm reaching for a specific goal. If you reach it, it's not interesting any more, and if you don't reach it, you get frustrated.'

Working as design director at Established & Sons, alongside his other venture The Wrong Shop, SEBASTIAN WRONG shares his views on his profession

WORDS
Enya Moore

PORTRAITS
Winter Vandenbrink

WHAT I'VE LEARNED

SEBASTIAN WRONG

1971
Born in London, United Kingdom

1993
Graduates as sculptor from the Camberwell School of Art

2003
Launches Spun Lamp for Flos

2005
Founding member of the British manufacturer Established & Sons

2011
Launches The Wrong Shop, an online platform that sells edition prints by notable designers and artists from around the world

2012
Leaves his position of design director of Established & Sons

2013
Founds WH (Wrong for HAY), conceived as a specialist lighting manufacturer

2016
WH has evolved into Wrong.London, dedicated entirely to lighting

2017
Returnes to Established & Sons as design director under new ownership

ABOVE **SPUN LIGHT FOR FLOS, 2003.**

OPPOSITE PAGE **HEIDI STOOL FOR ESTABLISHED & SONS, 2008.**

'I studied sculpture and specialized in metalwork and bronze-casting. After graduating I set up a small workshop in South London with a classmate. It was a squat, where we built a bronze-casting foundry, basically to play around with our ideas. It was very rough and ready, but also engaging and hands-on.'

'My break came when an American client asked me to reproduce a set of brass horn candelabras. I had to find a traditional horn maker, whom I eventually discovered in Norfolk, in the middle of nowhere. When I went to his workshop, I was intrigued by the tools he used to make trumpets and trombones. It gave me an idea for a lamp, which turned out to be the Spun Light, now manufactured by Flos.'

'At that time I was fabricating bits and pieces simply to earn a living. I wasn't interested in being a designer at all. I was much more enthusiastic about pursuing a career as a sculptor.'

'I learned a huge amount at Established & Sons — it was the best education I could have had in the business. When we launched in 2005, the design world was very different to what it is now. We were entering a whole new era of ideas and concepts. Art was merging with design, and there were a lot of opportunities to be more extravagant and indulgent. We embraced that spirit. It was a really important period for me. I wouldn't be where I am today without that experience.'

'In 2012 I left Established & Sons, only to return again five years later. When I am now commissioning designers whose work will be put into production, I place no emphasis at all on the person's name. I look at the merits of the design. Over the years, the business got a bit lost. It became too egocentric. Because of the strong focus on big-name designers, the value of the product was neglected.'

'I am a Londoner. From here, you can work with virtually anyone you want internationally. The city has so many different energies. It is very diverse and cosmopolitan, with a lot of cultural crossovers.'

Peer Lindgreen

'We don't need any
more chairs. Everything
we make is really surplus
to requirement'

'We're a bridge between
 different generations
 and cultures'

'My deepest regrets are designs that go nowhere. I am a designer; my currency is my design. When a product is stuck with a company that for whatever reason is unable to market it, produce it or invest in it — that's very frustrating. But it's the responsibility of the company, not the designer.'

'The job of a good designer is not just to design but to understand the *business* of design. The easy part is designing the object. The complicated part is getting that object into production. It's a big advantage to work with a designer who understands the complexity involved in the overall process and who actively offers assistance.'

'We don't need any more chairs. Everything we make is really surplus to requirement. In order to justify doing something new, it has to have some value. Young designers need to find that value in their ideas, to connect with it and to express it.'

Just over 50 years of age, **TOKUJIN YOSHIOKA** reflects on a life dedicated to producing poetic designs

WORDS
Kanae Hasegawa

PORTRAITS
Tada (Yukai)

OPPOSITE PAGE **HONEY-POP
CHAIR, 2000-01.**

FOLLOWING SPREAD LEFT
**RAINBOW CHURCH, MUSEUM OF
CONTEMPORARY ART, TOKYO,
2013-14.**

FOLLOWING SPREAD RIGHT
PRISM, 2017.

'I was brought up in a region called Saga. It's part of Kyushu Island, the most southwestern of Japan's four main islands. I spent my childhood in an environment far removed from the design world and the material cultures found in metropolises. If I had a pencil in my hand, I would get swept up in drawing.'

'I was absorbed by the art and science classes at school. At a young age, I was thrilled to discover that when you draw on paper with citrus juice and then apply heat, colour appears on the paper — it's like something a spy uses to send coded messages. Exploring how to manipulate such natural phenomena fascinated me. It gave me great delight to see my classmates mesmerized by what I was doing; that's the reason I was driven to continue making things that people enjoy. Besides that, I was a quiet boy.'

'When I was young, I couldn't imagine there being such a profession as *designer*. Back then, I associated the word with fashion designers, not furniture designers. I didn't think it was possible to make a living out of drawing and making things — activities that gave me pure joy.'

'I went to Kuwasawa Design School in Tokyo when I was a teenager. While there, I heard about designer Shiro Kuramata. His works gave me a new perspective on furniture design; they enlightened me. I wanted to become a creator with an attitude similar to Kuramata's. I was fortunate enough to work under him for a year. Then I was introduced to Issey Miyake, and I started working for him. Mr Miyake is also an unconventional designer. He encouraged me to explore new ways of making and allowed me to design the scenography and installation for his exhibition. But the design was for the Issey Miyake brand, so I thought: *what if Issey Mikaye were designing this*? It was about *his* identity, not my own self-expression.'

'My career changed course in 2000, when I established my own office. I had been nurturing some of my own ideas while working at Issey Miyake. My first project was the office itself, which I built from scratch rather than renting a furnished space. I brought in wooden beams and poles from a 150-year-old demolished rice granary in Shimane Prefecture in western Japan. I combined them with industrial materials, and at the time it was quite rare to mix old natural materials with modern industrial ones. The use of both was a statement to myself — the statement of a man looking towards the future while also being aware of the history of design. My work is firmly rooted in what I've learned from the past.'

'Honey-Pop, a chair I designed in 2000, represented a ground-breaking moment in my career. Realized in 2001, it was an exploration in making a chair with a honeycomb structure. Layers of two-dimensional paper unfold to form a three-dimensional object. I wanted to find

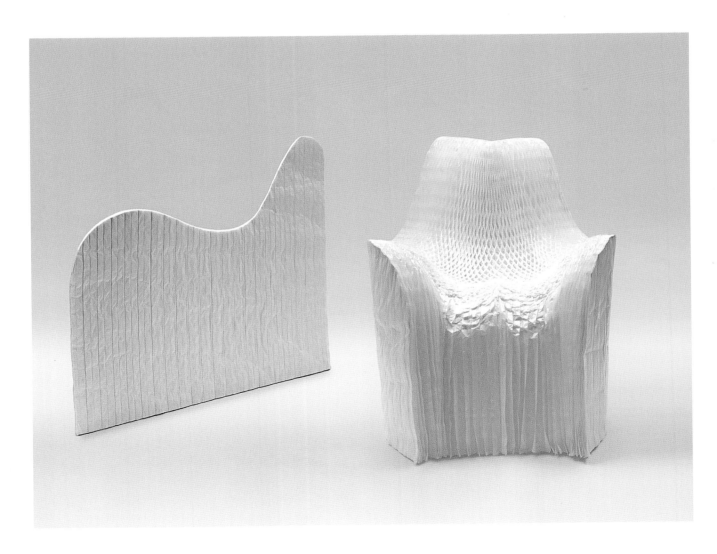

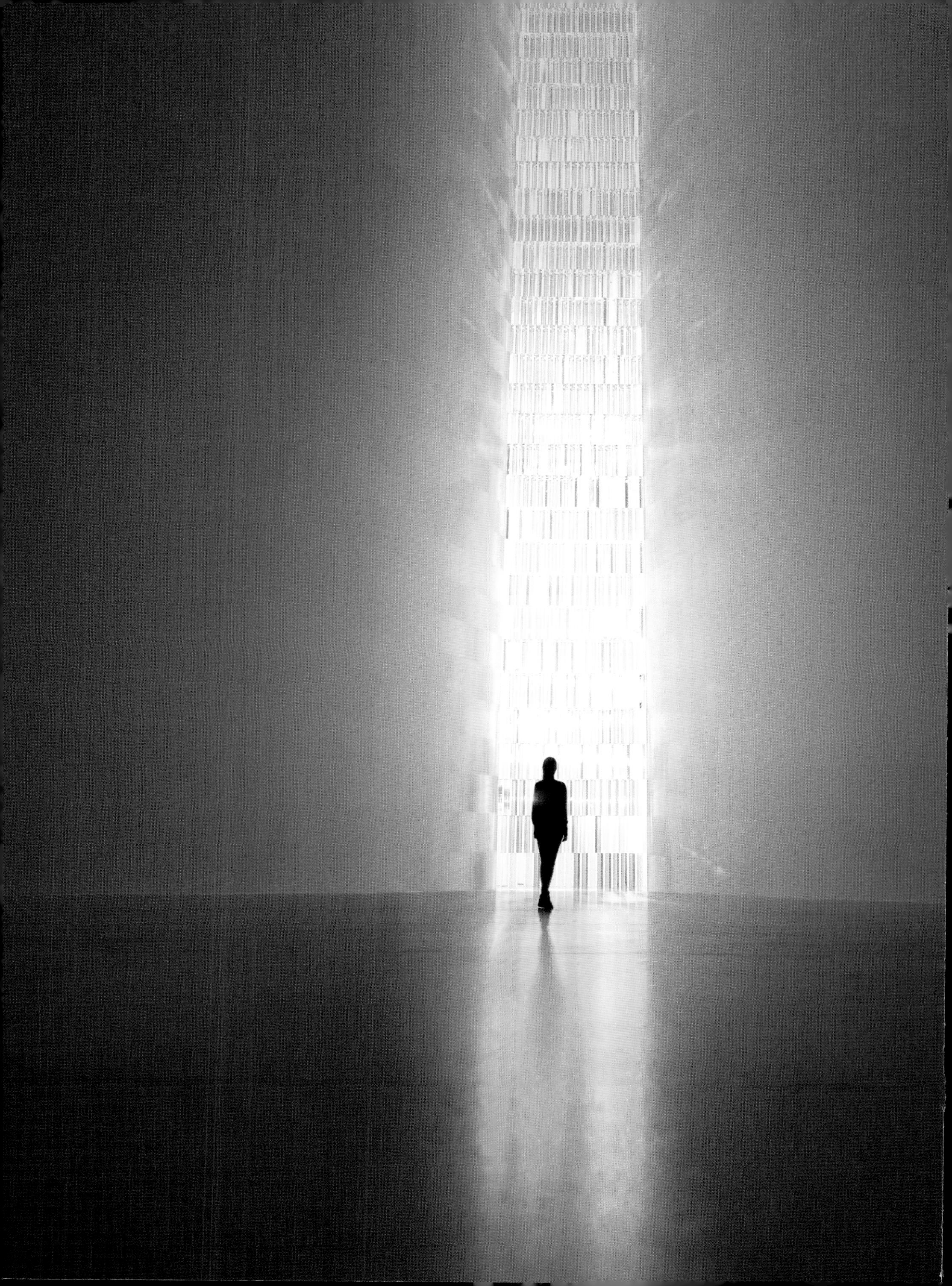

'I research the past and envision the future'

out how to make a chair in a brand-new way. It was my challenge to the chair and its history. I initially presented it at Milan Design Week, and it kick-started my career.'

'My work falls into two categories. One is for the industry and involves a client; in that case, my objective is to meet the client's needs. The second is personally initiated work; no one asks me to make it. I have stacks of drawings and sketches of ideas long in the making. They don't necessarily have to be realized.'

'I always try to create something that doesn't yet exist. The idea for Pane came about when I was considering how to make a chair without a conventional frame of wire or wood. Ultimately, I used bundles of thin polyester fibres to form the structure and to distribute the user's weight, while also offering comfort to the sitter. The chair was realized in 2006, but it took three years to develop.'

'I research the past and envision the future. But to realize my vision, I need craftspeople, engineers, manufacturers — the hands and skills of many. Because my designs are unprecedented, people don't know how to realize what they're looking at — they tell me what I'm trying to do is impossible. Earlier on in my career, people didn't want to go out on a limb for a young designer with no credentials. I couldn't direct them to do what I wanted, so I started by using my own hands. In a way, being told something is impossible can be the shortest way to get a project going. Gradually, people began to understand my passion and my ideas; they challenged themselves to overcome the obstacles and make it work.'

'My career as an independent designer spans more than 20 years. During that time, I've come to the conclusion that compromise doesn't help my work to be actualized. A trade-off may be important at some stage if you want your designs to be produced commercially. But for my personal work, no. Because there are already enough objects in the world, I always think about the significance of bringing out a new product — about whether what I'm making is really a milestone. Pursuing a project is the consequence of long reflection about its implica-

'I ALWAYS TRY TO CREATE SOMETHING THAT DOESN'T YET EXIST'

tions. I need to be insistent, almost obstinate, to achieve my intention, because a trade-off is a trade-off. Compromise results in a different outcome.'

'I look into many methods for realizing my products. The larger my stock of methods, the better chance I have of making what I've designed. My past experiments can be modified and applied to different projects.'

'*Why am I doing this? I'm not doing any productive work*: a thought that sometimes comes into my head when I'm deadlocked. I feel hopeless.'

'I don't necessarily intend to make new forms; I intend to evoke emotions, to touch people's senses and make them joyful. I like to think that design is a good way to do this.'

'As I designer, I'm not content to wait for clients to come to me — or even for someone to say that I can make whatever I want if it's also something for them. I don't want to face the ifs, ands or buts that go with the inability to realize an idea just because I wasn't commissioned to do it. I will do it myself if I think the idea is significant. That's why I proposed a plan — which includes stadium, logo and torch — for the 2020 Olympic Games in Tokyo. I'm not an architect, so my concept wasn't selected for the design of a new national stadium. But the Olympics aren't just a sporting event; they will change the social system. I simply wanted to present my idea for such an epic event.'

'In the end, I guess that more than mesmerizing *others*, I want to see the unseen *myself*.'

CREDITS

WHAT I'VE LEARNED Twenty-eight creatives
share career-defining insights

PUBLISHER
Frame Publishers

AUTHORS
Izabela Anna, Penny Craswell, Lilia Glanzmann,
Tim Groen, Leo Gullbring, Kanae Hasegawa,
Matthew Hurst, Jeroen Junte, David Keuning,
Floor Kuitert, Melanie Mendelewitsch, Enya
Moore, Shonquis Moreno, Jeannette Petrik, Jill
Diane Pope, Anna Sansom, Monica Zerboni

PORTRAIT PHOTOGRAPHY
Madoka Akiyama, Andrew Boyle, Antonio
Campanella, Carmen Chan, Valentin Fougeray,
Gene Glover, Hideaki Hamada, Olivier Hero,
Daniel Hofer, Mirjam Kluka, KlunderBie, Floor
Knaapen, Mark Mahaney, Andrew Meredith,
Elsbeth Struijk van Bergen, Fiona Torre, Winter
Vandenbrink, Marte Visser, Tada (Yukai)

COPY EDITING
InOtherWords (D'Laine Camp,
Donna de Vries-Hermansader)

PRODUCTION
David Keuning

GRAPHIC DESIGN
Zoe Bar-Pereg (Frame Publishers)

PREPRESS
Edward de Nijs

SPECIAL THANKS TO
The editors of *Frame* (Robert Thiemann,
Tracey Ingram, Floor Kuitert, Anouk Haegens)

TRADE DISTRIBUTION USA AND CANADA
Consortium Book Sales & Distribution, LLC.
34 Thirteenth Avenue NE, Suite 101,
Minneapolis, MN 55413-1007
United States
T +1 612 746 2600
T +1 800 283 3572 (orders)
F +1 612 746 2606

TRADE DISTRIBUTION BENELUX
Frame Publishers
Luchtvaartstraat 4
1059 CA Amsterdam
The Netherlands
distribution@frameweb.com
frameweb.com

TRADE DISTRIBUTION REST OF WORLD
Thames & Hudson Ltd
181A High Holborn
London WC1V 7QX
United Kingdom
T +44 20 7845 5000
F +44 20 7845 5050

ISBN 978-94-92311-26-9
© 2018 Frame Publishers, Amsterdam, 2018

Printed on acid-free paper produced from
chlorine-free pulp. TCF-certified.
Printed in Poland

987654321